T0222769

Rapid Game Development Using Cocos2d-JS

An end-to-end guide to 2D game development using JavaScript

Hemanth Kumar

Abdul Rahman

Apress®

Rapid Game Development Using Cocos2d-JS: An end-to-end guide to 2D game development using JavaScript

Hemanth Kumar
Chennai, Tamil Nadu, India

Abdul Rahman
Chennai, Tamil Nadu, India

ISBN-13 (pbk): 978-1-4842-2552-3
DOI 10.1007/978-1-4842-2553-0

ISBN-13 (electronic): 978-1-4842-2553-0

Library of Congress Control Number: 2016961533

Managing Director: Welmoed Spahr
Lead Editor: Pramila Balan
Technical Reviewer: Nakul Verma
Editorial Board: Steve Anglin, Pramila Balan, Laura Berendson, Aaron Black, Louise Corrigan, Jonathan Gennick, Robert Hutchinson, Celestin Suresh John, Nikhil Karkal, James Markham, Susan McDermott, Matthew Moodie, Natalie Pao, Gwenan Spearing
Coordinating Editor: Prachi Mehta
Copy Editor: April Rondeau
Compositor: SPi Global
Indexer: SPi Global
Artist: SPi Global

Distributed to the book trade worldwide by Springer Science+Business Media New York, 233 Spring Street, 6th Floor, New York, NY 10013. Phone 1-800-SPRINGER, fax (201) 348-4505, e-mail orders-ny@springer-sbm.com, or visit www.springeronline.com. Apress Media, LLC is a California LLC and the sole member (owner) is Springer Science + Business Media Finance Inc (SSBM Finance Inc). SSBM Finance Inc is a **Delaware** corporation.

For information on translations, please e-mail rights@apress.com, or visit www.apress.com.

Apress and friends of ED books may be purchased in bulk for academic, corporate, or promotional use. eBook versions and licenses are also available for most titles. For more information, reference our Special Bulk Sales–eBook Licensing web page at www.apress.com/bulk-sales.

Any source code or other supplementary materials referenced by the author in this text are available to readers at www.apress.com. For detailed information about how to locate your book's source code, go to www.apress.com/source-code/. Readers can also access source code at SpringerLink in the Supplementary Material section for each chapter.

Printed on acid-free paper

Contents at a Glance

Contents

About the Authors

Hemanth Kumar and **Abdul Rahman** are a team of full-stack JavaScript experts, researchers, and mobile game developers with a wide range of experience in Web and game development. They are well versed in Cocos2d-x, Unity3D, and building artificial intelligence for games. They are also experts in doing scalable architecture for high-traffic websites. Their main passion is video game development.

They are well versed in writing complex shaders for games, they published mobile games such as Blocky Pass, Little ninja town, Jumpo Jumpie on both android and ios, they have wrote several unity plugins as well, they are also good in android and ios native apps development and built several successful apps which are now used by millions of users world wide such as learn arabic basics for android and GXP (goals tracker for ios), they are also experts in OpenGL, WebGL, iOS Metal and Vulcan on android.

Hemanth is currently a web developer for a company and he builds games in his free time, listening to music, playing guitar, and watching movies are his hobbies.

Abdul is currently self employed and working on his dream app GXP (goals tracker for iOS), watching movies and bullying friends are his hobbies.

About the Technical Reviewer

Nakul Verma is a professional game developer currently working as a senior unity developer at Aquimo Sports Pvt Ltd. If you talk about the industry, then he has been in this field for around two years, but if you talk about passion and inclination, then he has been around for a decade. In these two years or so, he has worked on a variety of game genres using multiple technologies along the way. He has worked on a couple of casual puzzle games, an endless runner, an endless casual game, a couple of card games (*Rummy* on Cocos2d-JS and an African game), and a physics simulation sample, and is currently working independently on his own game that will be hitting the stores soon. The game technologies that he is proficient in are Unity, Cocos 2D-X/JS, Construct, and Allegro. Gaming has always been one of his favorite hobbies, along with sports, music, breakdancing, and a few more. Technology, gadgets, machines, and software have always fascinated him. He has always had the urge to learn more about the things that he likes, be it in the real world or in the virtual world, and to eventually be the best that he can be in them. His favorite game genres are first-person shooters, platformers, and puzzlers. When he is not making or playing games, he is either working out, breakdancing, or messing with some gadget around him.

He is a B.Tech graduate from PEC University of Technology in the field of electronics and electrical communication.

Acknowledgments

I would like to thank my sister, Priya, and my mom, Indrani, for supporting me in all situations. I also thank my dad, Krishnamurthy. Dad, remembering you is easy—I do it every day; missing you is heartache that never goes away!

—Hemanth Kumar

The completion of this undertaking could not have been possible without the participation and support of the following people

To my friend, Hemanth Kumar, my dad, Salam, my mom, Badrunnisa, my wife, Shameera Sultana, my son, Yusuf Omar, and all my relatives, friends, and mentors for their endless support, either morally, financially, or physically—thank you.

Above all, to the God Almighty, for bestowing knowledge and wisdom upon me.

—Abdul Rahman

CHAPTER 1

■ ■ ■

Getting Started

1.1 Introduction

In the early days, games were hard to make, but in recent years lots of 2D and 3D frameworks and tools have evolved that simplify game development and enable developers to produce high-quality games quickly. Cocos is a game engine that is widely used for making 2D games. Over the years, Cocos has established a solid foundation among developers. Many popular games in the market are made using Cocos. In 2010, Cocos2d-x, which is the C++ port of Cocos2D, was introduced. This enabled developers to make cross-platform 2D games. After that, Cocos2d-js, which is the JavaScript port of Cocos2d, was introduced, enabling developers to produce browser-based games as well as cross-platform native games that use JSB.

Cocos2D is the proven standard for making 2D games because of its simplicity and rich sets of features. In the coming sections, we are going to take a deep look at the Cocos2d-js framework and its features. By the end of this book, you will have a solid understanding of the Cocos2D-js framework, best practices, and the rich set of features that will enable you to develop your awesome game quickly.

Let's begin!

1.2 Environment Setup
1.2.1 Python Installation

Most of the time, you will be dealing with the Cocos console to create, run, compile, and deploy your project. The console uses Python. So, the first thing you need to do is to install Python. You can download it from the official Python site at `https://www.python.org/downloads/`.

If you are developing on MacOS X, it comes with Python installed by default.

Electronic supplementary material The online version of this chapter (doi:10.1007/978-1-4842-2553-0_1) contains supplementary material, which is available to authorized users.

H. Kumar and A. Rahman, *Rapid Game Development Using Cocos2d-JS*, DOI 10.1007/978-1-4842-2553-0_1

1.2.2   Cocos Console Setup

For Cocos2d-js, the development environment is actually a part of the Cocos console, so you have to download the Cocos2d-x bundle, or you may also go for the HTML5 Lite version if you wish to develop only for the Web.

1.2.2.1   Steps

- Download the cocos2d-x bundle from `https://cocos2d-x.org/ download`.

- Extract the zip file to your local drive.

- Open the terminal on Mac or the command prompt on Windows and navigate to the extracted folder.

- Run the following command:

```
1   python setup.py
```

- This will set up the Cocos console, which uses both Android and iOS environment settings, and update the environment variables.

1.3   Creating Your First App

Create a separate folder of your choice in your favorite location. It is good practice to keep all of your Cocos2d-js projects within one root folder.

Open the terminal and navigate to the created folder path, then execute the following commands:

- Cocos2d-js project:

```
1   cocos new sampleproject -l js
```

- Cocos2d-js project with web engine only:

```
1   cocos new sampleproject -l js --no-native
```

- Cocos2d-js project in specific directory:

```
1   cocos new sampleproject -l js -d ./Projects
```

`sampleproject` is the name of your project and `-l js` specifies the JavaScript language. This creates the "Hello World" sample, which you can use as the base for your game. For our purposes, we will modify this app to make our own "Hello World" screen. Before that, however, you should understand the folder structure that Cocos2d-js follows.

1.3.1   Folder Structure

When you create a new project, the Cocos console will create a folder structure like the one seen in Figure 1-1.

Figure 1-1. *Project folder structure*

- src - folder where you have all the JavaScript files for your game
- res - folder where you have all the images and other resources that are referenced in your game
- frameworks - folder where you have the actual Cocos2d-js engine, support files for native deployment, JSB, and so on. Apart from this, there are the configuration files project.json, which serves as the main meta configuration for the runtime for your game, and mainfest.webapp, which has configuration information related to the Web.

1.3.2   Structure of project.json

This file has meta information about your Cocos2d-js project. Let's have a look into the json structure.

```
 1   {
 2     "version": "1.0",
 3     "name": "sampleproject1",
 4     "description": "sampleproject1",
 5     "launch_path": "/index.html",
 6     "icons": {
 7       "128": "/res/icon.png"
 8     },
 9     "developer": {
10       "name": "Cocos2d-html5",
11       "url": "http://cocos2d-x.org/"
12     },
13     "default_locale": "en",
14     "installs_allowed_from": [
15       "*"
16     ],
17     "orientation": "portrait-primary",
18     "fullscreen": "true"
19   }
```

- version - your application version

- name - name of your application

- description - the description of your application

- launch_path - the startup HTML file for Cocos2d-js; used by the Cocos console when deploying/debugging your application as a Web app

- icons - application icons of various sizes; used by the Cocos console during native deployment

- developer - information about the developer of the application

- default_locale - default localization setting for your application; represents which language to use by default

- orientation - orientation profile to support

- fullscreen - used when deployed to native platforms

1.3.3 Code

If you open main.js, you will see the following code.

```
1   cc.game.onStart = function(){
2       //If referenced loading.js, please remove it
3       if(!cc.sys.isNative && document.getElementById("cocosLoading")) 4
4
5           document.body.removeChild(document.getElementById
            ("cocosLoading"));
6
7       // Pass true to enable retina display, disabled by default to
        improve perfor\
8       mance
9       cc.view.enableRetina(false);
10      // Adjust viewport meta
11      cc.view.adjustViewPort(true);
12      // Set up the resolution policy and design resolution size
13      cc.view.setDesignResolutionSize(800, 450, cc.ResolutionPolicy.
        SHOW_ALL);
14      // The game will be resized when browser size changes
15      cc.view.resizeWithBrowserSize(true);
16      //load resources
17      cc.LoaderScene.preload(g_resources, function () {
18          cc.director.runScene(new HelloWorldScene());
19      }, this);
20  };
21  cc.game.run();
```

The Cocos2d-js engine will begin by executing the onStart function, which has code to kickstart your game. There are a few configuration-related things going on in the preceding code that will be explained in later chapters. For now, we will focus on the cc. LoaderScene part.

```
1   cc.LoaderScene.preload(g_resources, function () {
2       cc.director.runScene(new HelloWorldScene());
3   }, this);
```

The preceding code loads the "Hello World" scene. cc.director is the single controller instance for your game. The purpose of this director is to guide your game through execution, loading and unloading the scene and getting information about the game-execution environment, such as screen size and so on. In this code, the director uses the runScene function to load the HelloWorldScene, which is loaded inside preload. preload loads the resources specified in g_resources into the Cocos cache, and once the resources have been loaded, a callback function is executed that has the code to load the HelloWorldScene.

Let's have look at HelloWorldScene and HelloWorldLayer. Open app.js inside src. At the bottom of app.js you will see code like this:

```
1    var HelloWorldScene = cc.Scene.extend({
2        onEnter:function () {
3            this._super();
4            var layer = new HelloWorldLayer();
5            this.addChild(layer);
6        }
7    });
```

A scene is told to run by invoking the onEnter function, and HelloWorldLayer is injected as a child of the scene.

We are going to modify HelloWorldLayer to make things simple.

```
1    var HelloWorldLayer = cc.Layer.extend({
2        sprite:null,
3        ctor:function () {
4            this._super();
5            var size = cc.winSize;
6            var helloLabel = new cc.LabelTTF("Hello World", "Arial", 38);
7            // position the label on the center of the screen
8            helloLabel.x = size.width / 2;
9            helloLabel.y = size.height / 2 + 200;
10           // add the label as a child to this layer
11           this.addChild(helloLabel, 5);
12
13           // add "HelloWorld" splash screen
14           this.sprite = new cc.Sprite(res.HelloWorld_png);
15           this.sprite.attr({
16               x: size.width / 2,
17               y: size.height / 2
18           });
19           this.addChild(this.sprite, 0);
20           return true;
21       }
22   });
```

This layer has two children; one is cc.LabelTTF, which has "Hello World" as text, and the other is a HelloWorld_png sprite. Throughout this book, we are going to use portrait screen resolution. So, in main.js, you should change the following line:

```
1    //This is landscape
2    cc.view.setDesignResolutionSize(800, 450, cc.ResolutionPolicy.SHOW_ALL);
```

to

```
1   //Swap the width and height so that it can be portrait
2   cc.view.setDesignResolutionSize(450, 800, cc.ResolutionPolicy.SHOW_ALL);
```

Width and height have been swapped.

1.4   Running "Hello World"

To make things simple, throughout this book we are going to run all the code in a
Web browser. However, deploying it on a device as a native app is your choice. To run
this sample type, navigate to the project path in the terminal and type the following
command:

```
1   cocos run -p web
```

This will launch the app in the browser; however, you can launch the app in Android,
iOS, or Windows phone by altering -p param as 'android' or 'ios'. You will see
something like what is shown in Figure 1-2.

Figure 1-2. Hello World

1.5   Example for This Book

All the example code for this book is available at `https://github.com/nutcrackify/` `Rapid_Game_Development_Using_Cocos2d-js`.

1.5.1   Running the Code Examples

There are many ways in which you can get the code examples up and running. We found the following steps made it easy to get the example code up and running quickly. Run the following commands in the terminal.

1.5.1.1   Steps

- Create a new Cocos2d-js project:

```
1   cocos new codeexamples -l js
```

- Navigate to the project folder in the terminal:

```
1   cd codeexamples
```

- Initialize an empty git repository:

```
1   git init
```

- Delete all the files and folders in the current folder except the `frameworks/` folder (see Figure 1-3).

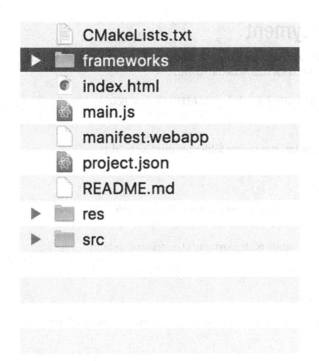

Figure 1-3. Hello World

- Add the remote (code samples repository) to the local git repository using either of the following commands:

```
1  (if you use ssh)
2  git remote add origin git@github.com:nutcrackify/Rapid_Game_Development_
   Using_Co\
3  cos2d-js.git
4
5  (if you use https)
6  git remote add origin https://github.com/nutcrackify/Rapid_Game_
   Development_Usin\
7  g_Cocos2d-js.git
```

- Pull the repository:

```
1  git pull origin master
```

- Run the example:

```
1  cocos run -p web
```

1.6 Native Deployment

Apart from on the Web, you may also deploy your Cocos2d-js samples to native platforms. The following is the command used for native deployment.

```
1  cocos deploy [-h] [-s SRC_DIR] [-q] [-p PLATFORM] [-m MODE]
```

- [-h] is help.

- [-s SRC_DIR] represents the source folder of your Cocos2d-js project.

- [-q] is quite mode.

- [-p PLATFORM] represents the target platform (i.e., Android, iOS, etc.)

- [-m MODE] represents mode of deployment (i.e., release, debug)

1.6.1 Android Setup

You can skip this part if you already have the Android environment or if you don't want to compile and deploy for Android.

1.6.1.1 Steps

- Install JDK from http://www.oracle.com/technetwork/java/javase/downloads/index.html.

- Download Android Studio or SDK and NDK from https://developer.android.com/sdk/index.html.

- Extract the SDK if you are not installing Android Studio.

- Extract the NDK and place it in the root of SDK, making sure that SDK and NDK are in same root folder.

- Install Apache ant from https://ant.apache.org/bindownload.cgi.

Run the following command in your local Cocos2d-x installation folder and provide the Android NDK and SDK paths:

```
1  python python.py
```

To deploy your project to Android, run the following command from the project folder via the terminal:

```
1  cocos deploy -p android -m release
```

1.6.2   iOS Setup

Install XCode from OS X app store. Use the following command for iOS deployment:

```
1   cocos deploy -p ios -m release
```

In the next chapter, we are going to look at engine architecture, so let's move on.

CHAPTER 2

■ ■ ■

Architecture Overview

2.1 Engine Architecture

Understanding the architecture of Cocos2d-js will give you a solid foundation for understanding the overall framework. This section will not cover the detailed architecture, which is beyond the scope of this book, but we will cover the necessary details that you need to be aware of in order to move forward. Cocos2d-js is a pure JavaScript-based game framework that runs on the browser stack. You can compile it as a Web app and run in on every browser; however, the API's and object's hierarchy are the same as for Cocos2d-x. So, with the help of JSB and SpiderMonkey, your JavaScript game code can be deployed as a native app that actually utilizes the core rendering pipeline of OpenGL/DirectX. Let's have a look at the architecture in Figure 2-1.

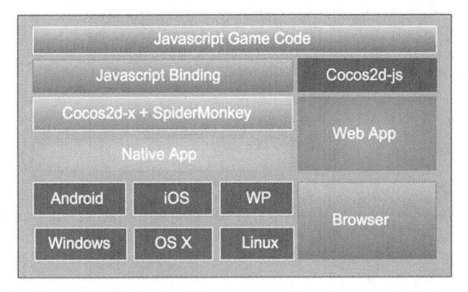

Figure 2-1. Cocos2d-js stack

© Hemanth Kumar 2016

H. Kumar and A. Rahman, *Rapid Game Development Using Cocos2d-JS*,
DOI 10.1007/978-1-4842-2553-0_2

As you can see, if your app is browser based, your JavaScript game code will utilize the library from Cocos2d-js and can be run like any other Web app. When you deploy this as native app using the Cocos console, your JavaScript code will be mapped to JavaScript bindings that actually point to native Cocos2d-x. Your JavaScript code will be converted to C by SpiderMonkey. So, Cocos2d-x will actually drive your JavaScript game.

2.2   JSB

As just mentioned, JSB contains mapping between JavaScript and C++ APIs of Cocos2d-x, so when you choose to deploy your game as a native app, all of your API usage is mapped to actual C++ API calls with the help of SpiderMonkey. Note that only documented Cocos2d-js APIs can be mapped to native API calls. If you try to invoke any functions internal to Cocos2d-js that are not documented, the app will work fine out of the box in the browser, but when you deploy it as a native app you may not see the same result. It is always recommended that you follow the documented APIs if you are planning to compile your game to any mobile platform.

2.3   Object Hierarchy

Cocos2d-js is based on object-oriented principles, so all the entities involved are considered classes and objects. Consider Figure 2-2.

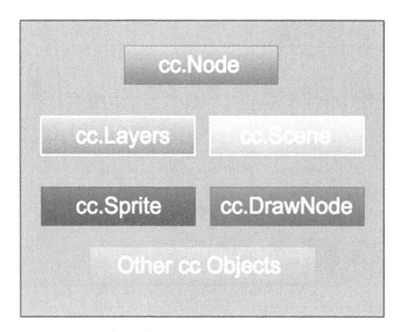

Figure 2-2.   Object hierarchy

Every class in Cocos2d-js, except for a few utilities, is inherited from cc.Node, from Scene and Layer to Sprites, all of which are instances of the Node object. Whenever you deal with any visible elements in Cocos2d-js, the topmost root object is cc.Node. So, most of the time you are dealing with a Node object. The derived objects will have their own behaviors and overrides based on their definitions and needs.

2.4   Deploy Options

As you are working with a pure JavaScript library, there are many more options for deploying your app than just relying on the Cocos console.

2.4.1   Deploy as Hybrid App

This option is subjected to your game's performance. If your game uses a heavy draw cycle, then this option is not recommended.

2.4.2   Deploy using Titanium

This option will enable you to deploy your app as a native app, but its feasibility may vary based on what you do in your games.

2.4.3   Cocos Console

This is the our recommended way to deploy your app to various platforms, but you can use other Cocos2d-x services such as SDKBOX, pluginX, and so on.

CHAPTER 3

■ ■ ■

A Deeper Look at Sprites

3.1 Introduction

Sprites are the most essential part of any 2D game. You will be dealing with this entity often while developing 2D games. In Cocos2d-js, this entity is defined by a class called cc.Sprite. In this section, we are going to explore this class in detail, including how it is organized, its usage, how to do frame animations, etc. So, let's begin.

3.2 Sprite Class

In Cocos2d-js, the cc.Sprite class is used to define the sprites of your game. This class can be initialized using the image file name, the initial rotation transformation, and so on. After that, you can update the x,y position dynamically based on your game logic. Let's see how this class is organized in Figure 3-1.

© Hemanth Kumar 2016
H. Kumar and A. Rahman, *Rapid Game Development Using Cocos2d-JS*,
DOI 10.1007/978-1-4842-2553-0_3

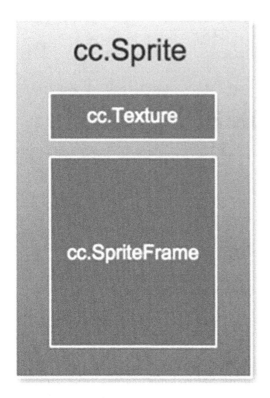

Figure 3-1. *Sprite class*

When you look into a sprite, it has two major parts. One is the texture, which represents the image, and the other is the sprite frame, which represents the `rect` in the texture image that is the current display of the sprite. Texture is represented by `cc.Texture` and the sprite frame is represented by `cc.SpriteFrame`. Let's have a look at a few examples.

3.3 Sprite with Single Image

In the `src` folder, create a file called `spriteimage.js` and copy and paste the following code:

```
1    var SpriteImageLayer = cc.Layer.extend({
2        sprite:null,
3        ctor:function () {
4            this._super();
5
6            var size = cc.winSize;
7
8            this.sprite = new cc.Sprite(res.Sprite_Image);
```

```
 9            this.sprite.attr({
10                 x: size.width / 2,
11                 y: size.height / 2
12            });
13            this.addChild(this.sprite, 0);
14            return true;
15       }
16   });
```

In project.json, include this new file, and in app.js, replace the existing layer instance in the scene with SpriteImageLayer.

```
1   var HelloWorldScene = cc.Scene.extend({
2       onEnter:function () {
3           this._super();
4           //Replace the layer with SpriteImageLayer.
5           var layer = new SpriteImageLayer();
6           this.addChild(layer);
7       }
8   });
```

In resources.js, the Sprite_Image property needs to be included; you can use the image of your choice.

```
1   var res = {
2       .......
3
4       Sprite_Image:"res/sprite_image.png"
5   };
```

I'll be using the image seen in Figure 3-2.

Figure 3-2. *sprite_image.png*

Remember these steps of running individual layers, since we will be creating separate layers for each example, and these steps will not be repeated in upcoming examples.

As you can see, the sprite has been initialized with a single image:

```
1    this.sprite = new cc.Sprite(res.Sprite_Image);
```

This constructor will create a cc.Texture instance with res.Sprite_Image, and cc. SpriteFrame will be initialized with rect(0,0,spriteWidth,spriteHeight) by default so as to show the full image. So, the output will be as in Figure 3-3.

Figure 3-3. *Sprite with single image*

3.3.1   FPS Display

The display at the bottom-left corner is called the FPS display, and it has three values:

- Draw calls
- Delta time
- Frame rate

You can control the visibility of the FPS display using the showFPS flag in project.json.

3.3.1.1 Draw Call

Renderings happen in draw calls, and for every single node in the scene there is an associated draw call. As draw calls increase, delta time and frame rate decrease, and this is directly proportional to the performance of the game.

3.3.1.2 Delta time

The time taken by the previous frame to complete its render.

3.3.1.3 Frame rate

Represents the number of frames rendered in a second.

3.4 Sprite with Sprite Sheet

To reduce the memory being used, you should pack all your assets into a single sprite sheet, which you will use through your game. For an individual sprite, the cc.SpriteFrame instance will define which portion of the sprite sheet needs to be shown in the display frame of the cc.Sprite instance. I'm going to use the sprite sheet shown in Figure 3-4 for the next example.

Figure 3-4. sprite_sheet.png

In src, create a file called spritesheet.js and copy the following code into it:

```
1   var SpriteSheetLayer = cc.Layer.extend({
2       sprite:null,
3       ctor:function () {
4
5           this._super();
6
7           var size = cc.winSize;
8
9           this.sprite = new cc.Sprite(res.Sprite_Sheet,
            cc.rect(438,93,67,94));
10          this.sprite.attr({
11              x: size.width / 2,
12              y: size.height / 2
13          });
14          this.addChild(this.sprite, 0);
15
16          return true;
17      }
18  });
```

Follow the steps in the previous example to include SpriteSheetLayer in HelloWorldScene. In resource.js, create a Sprite_Sheet variable and specify the sprite sheet's file name.

As you can see, a sprite is initialized with the sprite sheet as the texture and rect setting the current frame that needs to be displayed. See Figure 3-5.

Figure 3-5. *Sprite with sprite sheet*

The rect coordinates correspond to the last image of the first row in the sprite sheet.

3.5   Sprite Frame Animation

As explained before, cc.SpriteFrame is responsible for showing the current display of the image in cc.Sprite. This sprite frame can be changed at any point in time, which enables us to create frame-based animations. Let's look at an example. I'm going to use the same sprite sheet for this example.

In src, create a file called spriteanimation.js and copy the following code into it:

```
1   var SpriteAnimationLayer = cc.Layer.extend({
2       sprite:null,
3       ctor:function () {
4           ////////////////////////////////
5           // 1. super init first
6           this._super();
7
```

```
8              var size = cc.winSize;
9              //FrameData
10             var walk01 = cc.rect(0,0,72,97);
11             var walk02 = cc.rect(73,0,72,97);
12             var walk03 = cc.rect(146,0,72,97);
13             var walk04 = cc.rect(0,98,72,97);
14             var walk05 = cc.rect(73,98,72,97);
15             var walk06 = cc.rect(146,98,72,97);
16             var walk07 = cc.rect(219,0,72,97);
17             var walk08 = cc.rect(292,0,72,97);
18             var walk09 = cc.rect(219,98,72,97);
19             var walk10 = cc.rect(365,0,72,97);
20             var walk11 = cc.rect(292,98,72,97);
21
22             var frameDatas=[walk01,walk02,walk03,walk04,walk05,
23             walk06,walk07,walk08,walk09,walk10,walk11];
24             var texture = cc.textureCache.addImage(res.Sprite_Sheet);
25
26             //Create SpriteFrame and AnimationFrame with Frame Data
27             var animFrames=[];
28             for(var index in frameDatas)
29             {
30                 var spriteFrame = new cc.SpriteFrame(texture,
                   frameDatas[index]);
31                 var animFrame = new cc.AnimationFrame();
32                 animFrame.initWithSpriteFrame(spriteFrame, 1, null);
33                 animFrames.push(animFrame);
34             }
35
36             //Create an empty sprite
37             this.sprite = new cc.Sprite();
38             this.sprite.attr({
39                 x: size.width / 2,
40                 y: size.height / 2
41             });
42
43             this.addChild(this.sprite, 0);
44
45             var animation = cc.Animation.create(animFrames, 0.08);
46             var animate = cc.Animate.create(animation);
47
48             //Animate the sprite frame on the empty sprite
49             this.sprite.runAction(animate.repeatForever());
50
51             return true;
52         }
53    });
```

The idea behind the frame animation is that we are going to run through each frame in a specific time interval so that it will look like an animation sequence. In the preceding code, walk01 to walk11 represent frames with rects in the sprite sheet. If we put these frames together and run through it, it will look like a walking animation.

A SpriteFrame instance is created with this frame rect array (see Figure 3-6):

```
1   var texture = cc.textureCache.addImage(res.Sprite_Sheet);
2   var animFrames=[];
3   for(var index in frameDatas)
4   {
5       var spriteFrame = new cc.SpriteFrame(texture, frameDatas[index]);
6       var animFrame = new cc.AnimationFrame();
7       animFrame.initWithSpriteFrame(spriteFrame, 1, null);
8       animFrames.push(animFrame);
9   }
```

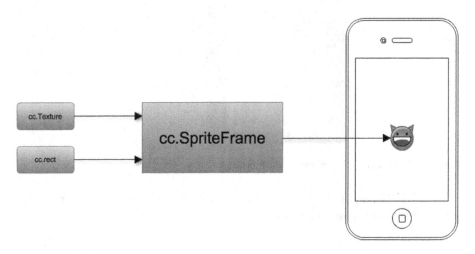

Figure 3-6. *SpriteFrame*

In this example, we are manually creating the cc.SpriteFrame instance, so it is going to need a texture instance of the sprite sheet. Thus, we added the sprite sheet to the texture cache, which returns the texture instance, which can be used to create all of the sprite frames.

Finally, the cc.Animation instance, which is used to perform the animation, is created using the list of images from cc.AnimationFrame with a time interval of 0.08 seconds.

The output will be a nice walk animation.

In the preceding case, frame data has been formed manually for a complete understanding of frame animation, but in reality the sprite sheet will be created from an individual image with the help of tools like TexturePack, and associated data files will be created. In the case of Cocos2d, it is a PList file that has all of the frame data related to the sprite sheet. In the next example, will see how to create the frame animation using PList.

3.6 Sprite Frame Animation with PList Data

We have created the same sprite sheet from an individual image using TexturePack, and we generated the PList file. See Figure 3-7.

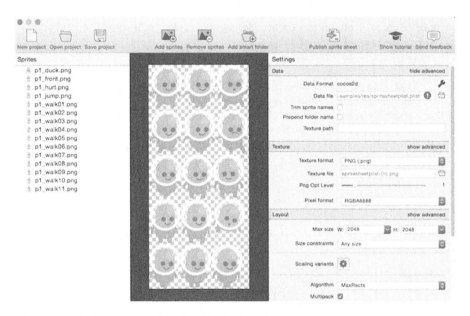

Figure 3-7. *TexturePack-generated sprite sheet*

While generating PList, make sure that you have selected the data format as Cocos2d. Figure 3-8 shows the generated texture.

Figure 3-8. *Sprite sheet from TexturePack*

You can examine the PList data file in the res folder of the sample project available at https://github.com/nutcrackify/Rapid_-Game_Development_Using_Cocos2d-js.

In src, create a file called plistanimation.js and copy the following code to it:

```
1   var PListAnimationLayer = cc.Layer.extend({
2       sprite:null,
3       ctor:function () {
4
5           this._super();
6
7           var size = cc.winSize;
8
```

```
9        cc.spriteFrameCache.addSpriteFrames(res.Sprite_Sheet1_P, res.
         Sprite_Shee\
10       t1);
11       //Create SpriteFrame and AnimationFrame with Frame Data
12       var animFrames=[];
13       for(var i=1;i<12;i++)
14       {
15            var str = "p1_walk" + (i < 10 ? ("0" + i) : i) + ".png";
16            var spriteFrame=cc.spriteFrameCache.getSpriteFrame(str);
17            animFrames.push(spriteFrame);
18       }
19
20       //Create an empty sprite
21       this.sprite = new cc.Sprite();
22       this.sprite.attr({
23            x: size.width / 2,
24            y: size.height / 2
25       });
26
27       this.addChild(this.sprite, 0);
28
29       var animation = new cc.Animation(animFrames, 0.08);
30       this.sprite.runAction(cc.animate(animation).repeatForever());
31
32       return true;
33     }
34   });
```

In resource.js, include the PList and sprite sheet file with variables Sprite_
Sheet1_P and Sprite_Sheet1; both have been added to the frame cache, as follows:

```
1   cc.spriteFrameCache.addSpriteFrames(res.Sprite_Sheet1_P, res.Sprite_
Sheet1);
```

Based on the PList data and sprite sheet, a sprite frame can be created using the
getSpriteFrame function, as follows:

```
1   var animFrames=[];
2   for(var i=1;i<12;i++)
3   {
4       var str = "p1_walk" + (i < 10 ? ("0" + i) : i) + ".png";
5       var spriteFrame=cc.spriteFrameCache.getSpriteFrame(str);
6       animFrames.push(spriteFrame);
7   }
```

Now we have list of sprite frames that can be animated using the `cc.Animation` class:

```
1  var animation = new cc.Animation(animFrames, 0.08);
2  this.sprite.runAction(cc.animate(animation).repeatForever());
```

This is the same walk animation that we did using the raw frame data without PList.

3.7   TextureCache with Sprites

Texture caches are an essential part of the sprite construct and are used to cache texture data in memory so that when the same texture is referred to again, it will be loaded from the cache. This improves the overall performance and in-memory optimization for your game. See Figure 3-9.

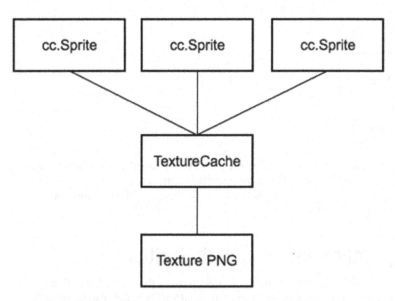

Figure 3-9. *Texture cache sprite*

Whenever you create a sprite with an image file, internally the image file gets loaded to TextureCache, and a Texture2D instance will be created with the data from TextureCache. In the previous code examples, you saw how we loaded the sprite sheets into the texture cache and used that to create a SpriteFrame instance. See Figure 3-10.

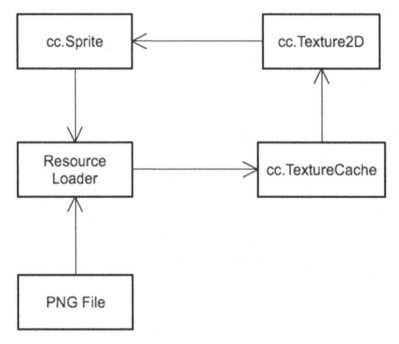

Figure 3-10. *Sprite with PNG*

The preceding figure represents the sprite with a single png file. Once the texture is returned from the resource loader it is cached into the texture cache, and the Texture2D instance is created from the cache data and used by cc.Sprite. This is the internal implementation of cc.Sprite.

3.8   SpriteFrameCache with Sprites

Similar to TextureCache, SpriteFrameCache is used to cache the SpriteFrame that is used by cc.Sprite. If you have a sprite sheet, individual SpriteFrames can be cached in SpriteFrameCache and used later whenever needed. This has been illustrated in the previous code samples and Figure 3-11.

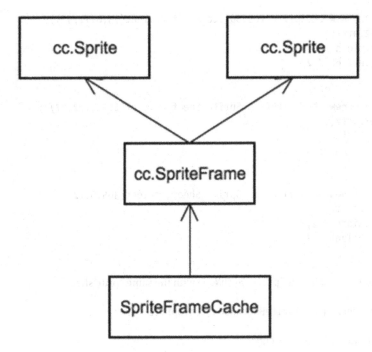

Figure 3-11. *SpriteFrameCache sharing SpriteFrame*

3.9 Sprite Batching

Sprite batching is a technique that combines multiple sprite renderings using a single draw call, provided that the sprites involved use the same texture or texture sheet.

3.9.1 SpriteBatchNode

cc.SpriteBatchNode is the sprite class used to combine multiple sprites into a single draw call, Let's have a look at an example.

First, let's create four individual sprites with the same sprite sheets and different SpriteFrame rects:

```
1   this.sprite1 = new cc.Sprite(res.Sprite_Sheet,cc.rect(438,93,67,94));
2   this.sprite1.attr({
3       x: size.width / 2,
4       y: size.height / 1.5
5   });
6
```

```
 7    this.sprite2 = new cc.Sprite(res.Sprite_Sheet,cc.rect(73,0,72,97));
 8    this.sprite2.attr({
 9        x: size.width / 2,
10        y: size.height / 2
11    });
12
13    this.sprite3 = new cc.Sprite(res.Sprite_Sheet,cc.rect(219,0,72,97));
14    this.sprite3.attr({
15        x: size.width / 2,
16        y: size.height / 3
17    });
18
19    this.sprite4 = new cc.Sprite(res.Sprite_Sheet,cc.rect(365,0,72,97));
20    this.sprite4.attr({
21        x: size.width / 2,
22        y: size.height / 5
23    });
```

Now, let's create an instance of SpriteBatchNode with the same sprite sheet:

```
 1    this.spritebatch=new cc.SpriteBatchNode(res.Sprite_Sheet);
```

Let's add sprites to the SpriteBatchNode:

```
 1    this.spritebatch.addChild(this.sprite1, 0);
 2    this.spritebatch.addChild(this.sprite2, 0);
 3    this.spritebatch.addChild(this.sprite3, 0);
 4    this.spritebatch.addChild(this.sprite4, 0);
```

Finally, let's add spritebatch to the layer:

```
 1    this.addChild(this.spritebatch);
```

Now, the full code is supposed to look like this:

```
 1    var SpriteBatchLayer = BaseSampleLayer.extend({
 2        sprite:null,
 3        ctor:function () {
 4
 5            this._super();
 6
 7            var size = cc.winSize;
 8
 9            this.sprite1 = new cc.Sprite(res.Sprite_Sheet,cc.
                 rect(438,93,67,94));
10            this.sprite1.attr({
11                x: size.width / 2,
```

```
12              y: size.height / 1.5
13          });
14
15          this.sprite2 = new cc.Sprite(res.Sprite_Sheet,
            cc.rect(73,0,72,97));
16          this.sprite2.attr({
17              x: size.width / 2,
18              y: size.height / 2
19          });
20
21          this.sprite3 = new cc.Sprite(res.Sprite_Sheet,cc.
            rect(219,0,72,97));
22          this.sprite3.attr({
23              x: size.width / 2,
24              y: size.height / 3
25          });
26
27          this.sprite4 = new cc.Sprite(res.Sprite_Sheet,
            cc.rect(365,0,72,97));
28          this.sprite4.attr({
29              x: size.width / 2,
30              y: size.height / 5
31          });
32          this.spritebatch=new cc.SpriteBatchNode(res.Sprite_Sheet);
33
34          this.spritebatch.addChild(this.sprite1, 0);
35          this.spritebatch.addChild(this.sprite2, 0);
36          this.spritebatch.addChild(this.sprite3, 0);
37          this.spritebatch.addChild(this.sprite4, 0);
38
39          this.addChild(this.spritebatch);
40
41          return true;
42      }
43  });
```

Note that all the sprites that belong to a single SpriteBatchNode must use the same instance of texture; also, SpriteBatchNode must contain a reference to the same texture. Otherwise, Cocos2d-js will not render the SpriteBatchNode.

The final output will look like that shown in Figure 3-12.

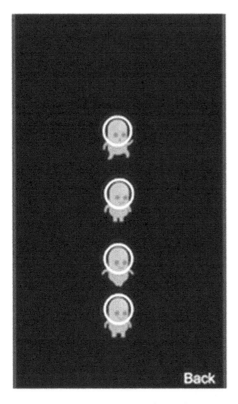

Figure 3-12. *SpriteBatchNode rendering*

However, the native renderer supports auto batching, which means if you are going for native deployment, sprite batching is supported automatically without the SpriteBatchNode.

3.10   Resolution Policies

Resolution policies are about adapting your game to different screen resolutions and profiles. Cocos2d-js offers sets of resolution policies with which to adapt your games. Without these, you have to manually scale up or down the content of your game based on the screen resolution.

There are two types of resolution policies: pre-defined policies and custom policies.

Pre-defined policies are offered by Cocos2d-js and are composed of various combinations of container and content strategies; they are supported in native deployments as well. With custom policies, you can define your own resolution policies with the combination of available containers and content strategies, but custom policies are supported only in Web deployments. Let's have a look.

3.10.1   Terminology

You need to aware of certain terms in order to fully understand resolution policies. You may already know that your game is hosted in canvas in your web-based Cocos2d-js game. See Figure 3-13.

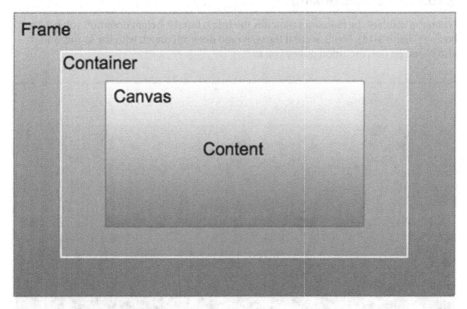

Figure 3-13. *Terminology used in resolution policies*

3.10.1.1   Frame

This represents the container outer to the canvas, usually a body element if you use the default index.html generated by the Cocos console.

3.10.1.2   Container

Cocos2d-js wraps your canvas in an div element, and that wrapped content is then again added to the original container element of canvas.

3.10.1.3   Content

Everything inside the canvas which is not part of dom.

3.10.1.4   Viewport

Viewport represents the world rect of canvas; it is canvas coordinates in pixels.

3.10.1.5   Letter Boxing

When the width of the container matches the frame but the height does not, you get letter boxing (Figure 3-14). It will occur if the w/h ratio does not match with the frame, and is also based on the resolution policy you use.

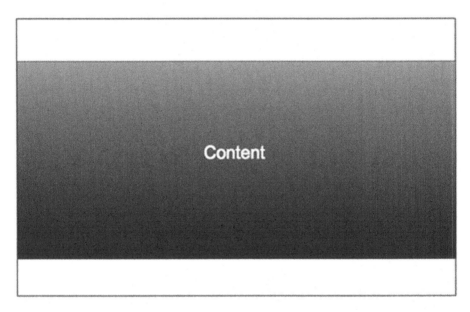

Figure 3-14. *Letter boxing*

3.10.1.6   Pillar Boxing

When height of the container matches the height of the frame but the width does not, you get pillar boxing (see Figure 3-15). The reason for this occurrence is the same as for letter boxing.

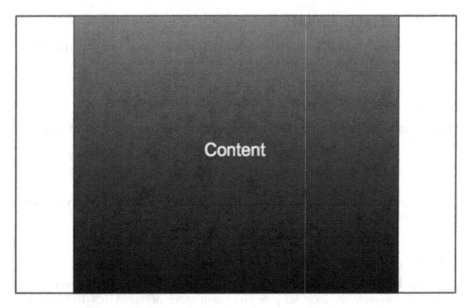

Figure 3-15. *Pillar Boxing*

3.10.2   Pre-defined Resolution Policies

There are five predefined policies offered by Cocos2d-js, which we will now discuss.

3.10.2.1   SHOW_ALL

This will scale up the container to the maximum size within the container bounds; all the contents in current scene will be visible.

3.10.2.2   NO_BORDER

This will scale up the container to fill the frame so that there won't be any visible area in frame while maintaining the proportion of provided width and height.

3.10.2.3   EXACT_FIT

This will scale the container to fit into the frame. Note that the provided width and height ratio won't be maintained.

3.10.2.4   FIXED_WIDTH

This will scale the width of the container to match the width of the frame and scale the height to match the w/h ratio. You may see letter boxing, if w/h ratio won't match.

3.10.2.5 FIXED_HEIGHT

This will scale the height of the container to match the frame's height and scale the width to match the w/h ratio. You may see pillar boxing, if w/h ratio won't match.

3.10.3 How to Use

In the file `main.js`, there is a `cc.game.onStart` callback. You have to use the following line of code to set the resolution profile:

```
1   cc.view.setDesignResolutionSize(320, 480, cc.RESOLUTION_POLICY.SHOW_ALL);
```

The first two parameters are width and height, which is the aspect ratio of your game, and the third is the resolution policy.

3.10.4 Custom Resolution Policies

As we seen before, pre-defined policies are a combination of container and content strategy. For example, the `SHOW_ALL` policy is a combination of `PROPORTION_TO_FRAME` and `SHOW_ALL`, as follows:

```
1       cc.RESOLUTION_POLICY.SHOW_ALL = new cc.ResolutionPolicy
        (cc.ContainerStrategy\
2   .PROPORTION_TO_FRAME, cc.ContentStrategy.SHOW_ALL);
```

This is the internal implementation of `SHOW_ALL`. You can define your own policies with a combination of pre-defined container and content strategy.

3.10.5 Pre-defined Container Strategies

- `cc.ContainerStrategy.EQUAL_TO_FRAME`
- `cc.ContainerStrategy.PROPORTION_TO_FRAME`
- `cc.ContainerStrategy.ORIGINAL_CONTAINER`

3.10.6 Pre-defined Content Strategies

- `cc.ContentStrategy.SHOW_ALL`
- `cc.ContentStrategy.NO_BORDER`
- `cc.ContentStrategy.EXACT_FIT`
- `cc.ContentStrategy.FIXED_WIDTH`
- `cc.ContentStrategy.FIXED_HEIGHT`

It is possible to create containers and content strategies of your own; all you have to do is use sub-classes cc.ContainerStrategy and cc.ContentStrategy and override the methods shown next.

3.10.7   For a Custom Container Strategy

```
1   var CustomContainerStrategy = cc.ContainerStrategy.extend({
2       preApply: function (view) {
3           // This function is called before the process of adaptation,
4           // you can remove this function if you don't need
5       },
6
7       apply: function (view, designedResolution) {
8           // Apply process
9       },
10
11      postApply: function (view) {
12          // This function is called after the process of adaptation,
13          // you can remove this function if you don't need
14      }
15  });
```

3.10.8   For Custom Content Strategy

```
1       var CustomContentStrategy = cc.ContentStrategy.extend({
2           preApply: function (view){
3               // This function is called before the process of
                   adaptation,
4               // you can remove this function if you don't need
5           },
6
7           apply: function (view, designedResolution) {
8               var containerW = cc.canvas.width, containerH = cc.canvas.
                   height;
9
10              // The process to calculate the content size, the x axe
                   scale and th\
11                 e y axe scale
12
13              return this._buildResult(containerW, containerH, contentW,
                contentH,\
14              scaleX, scaleY);
15          },
16
```

```
17          postApply: function (view) {
18              // This function is called after the process of
                   adaptation,
19              // you can remove this function if you don't need
20          }
21    });
```

You have to implement the apply function on both. You have access to frame, container, and content width and height.

CHAPTER 4

Handling Inputs and Events

4.1   Introduction

Handling user input is an essential part of any game. In Cocos2d-js, user input, such as by touch, mouse, or keyboard, is available in the form of events. There are three major parts involved in the event mechanism (see Figure 4-1):.

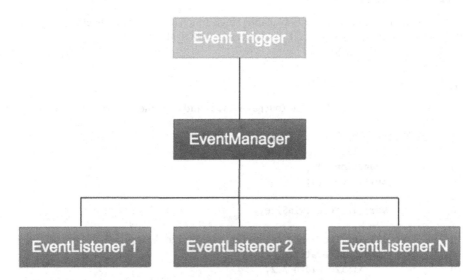

Figure 4-1. *Event mechanism in Cocos2d-JS*

© Hemanth Kumar 2016
H. Kumar and A. Rahman, *Rapid Game Development Using Cocos2d-JS*,
DOI 10.1007/978-1-4842-2553-0_4

4.1.1 Event Trigger

An event trigger is the source of any event. When a touch or any other input happens, the Cocos2d-js system will trigger an event in response.

4.1.2 Event Manager

When any event is triggered, event manager will get notified, EventManager is a singleton instance that is part of the Cocos2d-js system; it manages all the events.

4.1.3 Event Listeners

This is where the actual event-handling logic goes. Event manager will dispatch the events to all the event listeners and they will be handled by event listener instances.

4.2 Touch Events

There are two kind of touch events available: single touch (cc.EventListener.TOUCH_-ONE_BY_ONE) and multi-touch (cc.EventListener.TOUCH_ALL_AT_ONCE)

4.2.1 Single Touch

In the src folder, create a file called touchevents.js and copy the following code there:

```
1    var TouchEventsLayer = cc.Layer.extend({
2        sprite:null,
3        ctor:function () {
4            this._super();
5
6            var size = cc.winSize;
7
8            this.sprite = new cc.Sprite(res.Sprite_Image);
9            this.sprite.attr({
10               x:size.width / 2,
11               y:size.height / 2
12           });
13           this.addChild(this.sprite, 0);
14           this.sprite.tag='TouchTarget';
15
16           //Creating Event Listener Object
17           var listener = cc.EventListener.create({
18               event: cc.EventListener.TOUCH_ONE_BY_ONE,
19             swallowTouches: true,
20
```

```
21              onTouchBegan: function (touch, event) {
22                  var target = event.getCurrentTarget();
23                  var locationInNode = target.convertToNodeSpace(touch.
                    getLocation\
24  ());
25                  var s = target.getContentSize();
26                  var rect = cc.rect(0, 0, s.width, s.height);
27
28                      //Check the click area
29                  if (cc.rectContainsPoint(rect, locationInNode)) {
30                      cc.log('Touch began: Inside the sprite');
31                      //True has been returned to initiate the
                        OnTouchMove
32                      return true;
33                  }
34                  cc.log('Touch began: Outside the sprite');
35                  return false;
36              },
37              onTouchMoved: function (touch, event) {
38                  var target = event.getCurrentTarget();
39                  target.setPosition(touch.getLocation());
40              },
41              onTouchEnded: function (touch, event) {
42                  cc.log('Touch end');
43              }
44          });
45
46          //Added Event Listener To Sprite
47          cc.eventManager.addListener(listener, this.sprite);
48          return true;
49      }
50  });
```

In this example, the sprite can be dragged using single touch. The event listener is created using the event name cc.EventListener.TOUCH_ONE_BY_ONE, with swallowTouches set to true. When multiple event listeners are attached to the same target for the same event name, the first listener with swallowTouches: true will swallow the event, and it will not be passed on to the next listener.

```
1   cc.eventManager.addListener(listener, this.sprite);
```

In this case, even though a sprite is the target, a touch event will happen for every tap on the screen. To confirm that a touch has happened inside the sprite, the following code has been written:

```
1   var target = event.getCurrentTarget();
2   var locationInNode = target.convertToNodeSpace(touch.getLocation());
3   var s = target.getContentSize();
```

```
4    var rect = cc.rect(0, 0, s.width, s.height);
5
6    //Check the click area
7    if (cc.rectContainsPoint(rect, locationInNode)) {
8      cc.log('Touch began: Inside the sprite');
9      //True has been returned to initiate the OnTouchMove
10     return true;
11   }
```

In onTouchBegan, a condition has been checked as to whether a touch has happened within the sprite or not. If the touch is within the sprite, then true will be returned so that the touch move's gestures will be directed to the onTouchMoved function; the target position is changed as per the touch move.

4.2.2 Multi-Touch

Multi-touch event listeners can be created using event name cc.EventListener.TOUCH_ALL_AT_ONCE. Refer to the code snippet that follows:

```
1    var listener = cc.EventListener.create({
2        event: cc.EventListener.TOUCH_ALL_AT_ONCE,
3        swallowTouch: true,
4        onTouchesBegan: function (touches, event) {
5            .......
6        },
7        onTouchesMoved: function (touches, event) {
8            .......
9    },
10       onTouchesEnded: function (touches, event) {
11           .......
12       }
13   });
```

So, the callback for multi-touch is different from that for single touch. It has onTouchesBegan, onTouchesMoved, and onTouchesEnded functions. The touches object will have details about each touch, with touch ID. Mostly, multi-touch can be used in scenarios like map zoom, multi-touch for play control, and so on.

4.3 Mouse Events

As with touch events, mouse events are referred to by event name cc.EventListener.MOUSE. In the src folder, create a file called mouseevents.js and copy the following code into it:

```
1    var MouseEventsLayer = cc.Layer.extend({
2        sprite:null,
3        ctor:function () {
```

```
 4          this._super();
 5
 6          var size = cc.winSize;
 7
 8          this.sprite = new cc.Sprite(res.Sprite_Image);
 9          this.sprite.attr({
10              x: size.width / 2,
11              y: size.height / 2
12          });
13          this.addChild(this.sprite, 0);
14          this.sprite.tag='TouchTarget';
15
16          //Creating Event Listener Object
17          var listener = cc.EventListener.create({
18              event: cc.EventListener.MOUSE,
19                  swallowTouches: true,
20                  ismousedown:false,
21              onMouseDown: function (event) {
22                  var target = event.getCurrentTarget();
23                  var locationInNode = target.convertToNodeSpace(event.
                    getLocation\
24  ());
25                  var s = target.getContentSize();
26                  var rect = cc.rect(0, 0, s.width, s.height);
27
28                          //Check the click area
29                  if (cc.rectContainsPoint(rect, locationInNode)) {
30                      cc.log('Mouse Down: Inside the sprite');
31                      this.ismousedown=true;
32                  }
33                  cc.log('Mouse Down: Outside the sprite');
34                  return false;
35              },
36              onMouseMove: function (event) {
37                  if(this.ismousedown)
38                  {
39                      var target = event.getCurrentTarget();
40                      target.setPosition(event.getLocation());
41                  }
42              },
43              onMouseUp: function (event) {
44                  cc.log('Mouse Up');
45                  this.ismousedown=false;
46              }
47          });
48
```

```
49          //Added Event Listener To Sprite
50          cc.eventManager.addListener(listener, this.sprite);
51          return true;
52      }
53  });
```

In this example also, the sprite can be dragged with a mouse click, though there is one major difference between touch and mouse event handling. In touch, the onTouchBegan function has to return true in order to process onTouchMove. In mouse events, onMouseMove doesn't depend on the return value of onMouseDown. Both events can be processed simultaneously. To keep track of when a click has been made within the sprite, we have introduced the ismousedown flag. When a mouse down event happens within the sprite, the position will be changed via onMouseMove.

4.4   Keyboard Events

In the src folder, create a file called keyboardevent.js and copy the following code into it:

```
1   var KeyboardEventsLayer = cc.Layer.extend({
2       sprite:null,
3       ctor:function () {
4           this._super();
5
6           var size = cc.winSize;
7           var KeyCode={
8               LEFT:37,
9               UP:38,
10              RIGHT:39,
11              DOWN:40
12          };
13          var MoveOffSet=20;
14          this.sprite = new cc.Sprite(res.Sprite_Image);
15          this.sprite.attr({
16              x: size.width / 2,
17              y: size.height / 2
18          });
19          this.addChild(this.sprite, 0);
20          this.sprite.tag='TouchTarget';
21
22          //Creating Event Listener Object
23          var listener = cc.EventListener.create({
24              event: cc.EventListener.KEYBOARD,
25                  swallowTouches: true,
26              onKeyPressed: function (keyCode,event) {
```

```
27              var target = event.getCurrentTarget();
28              var position=target.getPosition();
29              switch(keyCode)
30              {
31                  case KeyCode.LEFT:
32                  position.x-=MoveOffSet;
33                  break;
34
35                  case KeyCode.RIGHT:
36                  position.x+=MoveOffSet;
37                  break;
38
39                  case KeyCode.UP:
40                  position.y+=MoveOffSet;
41                  break;
42
43                  case KeyCode.DOWN:
44                  position.y-=MoveOffSet;
45                  break;
46              }
47              target.setPosition(position);
48          },
49          onKeyReleased: function (event) {
50              cc.log('Key released');
51          }
52      });
53
54      //Added Event Listener To Sprite
55      cc.eventManager.addListener(listener, this.sprite);
56      return true;
57      }
58  });
```

In the preceding code, the same sprite drag is performed using UP, DOWN, LEFT, RIGHT key combinations. The onKeyPress function keycode is checked, and if the keycode is any of the arrow keys, the x,y position of the sprite is moved accordingly.

4.5   Accelerometer Events

Accelerometer events are referred to by the event name cc.EventListener. ACCELERATION. Accelerometer input needs to be enabled via input manager, as follows:

```
1   cc.inputManager.setAccelerometerEnabled(true);
```

After that, you can create a listener and attach it to the sprite using eventManager:

```
1   cc.eventManager.addListener({
2       event: cc.EventListener.ACCELERATION,
3       callback: function(acc, event){
4           // Processing logic here
5       }
6   }, sprite);
```

4.6   Custom Events

Apart from system-defined events, we can create our own events. See the following code snippet:

```
1   var listener = cc.EventListener.create({
2       event: cc.EventListener.CUSTOM,
3       eventName: "my_custom_event",
4       callback: function(event){
5           cc.log("Custom event 1 received, " + event.getUserData() +
            "times");
6       }
7   });
8   cc.eventManager.addListener(listener, 1);
```

This custom event has only one callback function, which will be invoked after the event is triggered:

```
1   var event = new cc.EventCustom("my_custom_event");
2   event.setUserData(counter.toString());
3   cc.eventManager.dispatchEvent(event);
```

The dispatchEvent function of the event manager is used to trigger the custom event. This method is also used internally to trigger the user-input events by the Cocos2d engine.

CHAPTER 5

■ ■ ■

Adding a GUI

5.1 Introduction

A GUI is another essential part of any game. It shows the HUD display, score, any required text, and buttons such as play and pause. Cocos2d-js has pre-defined node types to represent such GUI elements. Let's look at them one by one.

5.2 Labels

If you want to display any text in your game, then Label objects can be used. There are two types of label offered by Cocos2d-js.

5.2.1 Label with True Type Font

You can define a label such that it uses custom true type fonts. Usually, these fonts have a .ttf file format. In Cocos2d-js, the cc.LabelTTF class can be used to create such a label. Let's have a look at the syntax:

```
1   var label= new cc.LabelTTF(text, fontName, fontSize, dimensions,
    hAlignment, vAl\
2   ignment);
```

- [string] text - represents the text you want to display

- [string] fontName - represents the loaded .ttf font name

- [Number] fontSize - represents font size

- [cc.Size] dimensions - represents label width and height; if not set, this is calculated automatically

- hAlignment - represents horizontal alignment of text inside the label; it can be one of the following values: {cc.TEXT_ALIGNMENT_LEFT | cc.TEXT_ALIGNMENT_CENTER | cc.TEXT_ALIGNMENT_RIGHT}

© Hemanth Kumar 2016
H. Kumar and A. Rahman, *Rapid Game Development Using Cocos2d-JS*,
DOI 10.1007/978-1-4842-2553-0_5

- vAlignment - represents vertical alignment of text inside the
  label; it can be one of the following values: {cc.VERTICAL_TEXT_
  ALIGNMENT_TOP|cc.VERTICAL_TEXT_ALIGN-MENT_CENTER|cc.
  VERTICAL_TEXT_ALIGNMENT_BOTTOM}

All of these values can be changed dynamically using the appropriate set of
functions. Please refer to the documentation for more information on these functions.
You will see real examples in an upcoming section.

5.2.2   Label with Bitmap Font

In a bitmap font, each character is represented by an image. All the characters should be
located in one png file, and info regarding the font will be present in a (.fnt) file. The cc.
LabelBMFont class is used to represent this label type. Let's have look at its syntax:

```
1  var label = new cc.LabelBMFont(text, fntFile, width, alignment,
   imageOffset)
```

- [string] text - represents the text you want to display

- [fntFile] fntFile - represents the .fnt filename

- [width] width - represents the width of the label

- alignment – represents the horizontal alignment of the image
  label. Can be one of the following values: {cc.TEXT_ALIGNMENT_
  LEFT|cc.TEXT_ALIGNMENT_CENTER|cc.TEXT_-ALIGNMENT_RIGHT}

- [cc.point] imageOffset – represents the x,y offset point where
  the image center needs to be aligned

5.2.3   Example

In the src folder, create a file called labeldemo.js and copy the following code into it:

```
1   var LabelDemoLayer = cc.Layer.extend({
2       sprite:null,
3       ctor:function () {
4           this._super();
5
6           var size = cc.winSize;
7
8           var colorLayer = new cc.LayerColor(cc.color(142,29,42));
9           this.addChild(colorLayer);
10
11          this.Label1 = new cc.LabelTTF('Default Font Label','', 32);
```

```
12          this.Label1.attr({
13              x: size.width / 2,
14              y: size.height / 1.3
15          });
16          this.addChild(this.Label1);
17
18          this.Label2 = new cc.LabelTTF('Custom Font Label','Abduction',
            32);
19          this.Label2.attr({
20              x: size.width / 2,
21              y: size.height / 1.5
22          });
23          this.addChild(this.Label2);
24
25          this.Label3 = new cc.LabelTTF('Label With Stroke','Abduction',
            32);
26          this.Label3.attr({
27              x: size.width / 2,
28              y: size.height / 1.9
29          });
30          this.Label3.enableStroke(cc.color(0,0,0),10);
31          this.addChild(this.Label3);
32
33          this.Label4 = new cc.LabelTTF('Label With Shadow','Abduction',
            32);
34          this.Label4.attr({
35              x: size.width / 2,
36              y: size.height / 2.3
37          });
38          this.Label4.enableShadow(cc.color(0,0,0), 50, 50);
39          this.addChild(this.Label4);
40
41          this.Label5 = new cc.LabelBMFont("Bitmap Font", res.BM_Font);
42          this.Label5.attr({
43              x: size.width / 2,
44              y: size.height / 2.9
45          });
46          this.addChild(this.Label5);
47
48          return true;
49      }
50  });
```

As usual, do the steps to run this layer. Let's see how the label has been used. At first, cc.LayerColor has been included as a child so as to set the background color:

```
1   var colorLayer = new cc.LayerColor(cc.color(142,29,42));
2   this.addChild(colorLayer);
```

The first label is created using text 'Default font name', and fontname is specified as an empty string so that the label falls back to the default font in the system.

The second label is created with a loaded font name; in this case, I have used Abduction.ttf, which is specified in resource.js as follows:

```
1  var res = {
2     .....
3     Custom_TTF:"res/Abduction.ttf",
4     .....
5  };
```

So, during the app load, this font will be loaded into memory along with other resources in the res object:

```
1  this.Label2 = new cc.LabelTTF('Custom Font Label','Abduction', 32);
2  this.Label2.attr({
3     x: size.width / 2,
4     y: size.height / 1.5
5  });
6  this.addChild(this.Label2);
```

Specifying the font name 'Abduction' happens in the second parameter. Specifying the font filename directly in the label will not work.

The third label uses the same custom font 'Abduction'; the difference is that it enables a stroke on the label:

```
1  this.Label3.enableStroke(cc.color(0,0,0),10);
```

The first parameter is the color of the stroke, and the second is size.

The fourth label is created with shadow enabled using the following code:

```
1  this.Label4.enableShadow(cc.color(0,0,0), 50, 50);
```

Here, the first parameter is the color of the shadow, the second is the shadow offset from the label, and third is shadow size.

Finally, the fifth label is created with a bitmap font:

```
1  this.Label5 = new cc.LabelBMFont("Bitmap Font", res.BM_Font);
2  this.Label5.attr({
3     x: size.width / 2,
4     y: size.height / 2.9
5  });
6  this.addChild(this.Label5);
```

As with the second label, I have specified the font filename itself in the second parameter in resource.js BM_Font and BM_Font_Png, as follows:

```
1   var res = {
2       ....
3       BM_Font:"res/bitmapFontTest.fnt",
4       BM_Font_Png:"res/bitmapFontTest.png",
5       ....
6   };
```

As you can see, for bitmap fonts the associated .png file needs to be loaded along with a .fnt file. See an example of labels in Figure 5-1.

Figure 5-1. Labels in Cocos2d-js

5.3 Menu and MenuItem

In Cocos2d-js, there is a menu-based GUI that is defined by cc.Menu and cc.MenuItem, where cc.MenuItem should be the child of cc.Menu. CC.MenuItem is an abstract class, and there are three types of menu item available to be inherited from it.

5.3.1 MenuItemLabel

Any cc.Label instance can be used in this menu item type. The following is the syntax:

```
1  var menuitemLabel = new cc.MenuItemLabel(label,selector,target);
```

- [cc.Label] label - instance of cc.Label
- [string] selector - callback method name as string
- [object] target - object that has the selector function

5.3.2 MenuItemImage

An image can be used along with this menu item. The following is the syntax:

```
1  var menuItem = new cc.MenuItemImage(normalImage, selectedImage,
disabledImage, s\
2  elector, target);
```

- [string] normalImage - image file path that represents normal state
- [string] selectedImage - image file path that represents selected state
- [string] disabledImage - image file path that represents disabled state
- [string] selector - callback function name when menu item is clicked
- [object] target - object that has a selector callback function.

Let's have a look at an example.

5.3.3 Example

In the src folder, create a file called menuitem.js and copy the following code into it:

```
1  var MenuDemoLayer = cc.Layer.extend({
2      sprite:null,
3      ctor:function () {
```

```
4            this._super();
5
6            var size = cc.winSize;
7
8            var colorLayer = new cc.LayerColor(cc.color(142,29,42));
9            this.addChild(colorLayer)
10
11           this.Menu=new cc.Menu();
12           this.Menu.attr({
13               x: 0,
14               y: 0
15           });
16
17           //Menu item with label
18           var label=new cc.LabelTTF('MenuItem with label',36);
19           this.MenuItem1 = new cc.MenuItemLabel(label,'onMenuClicked',th
is);
20           this.MenuItem1.attr({
21               x: size.width / 2,
22               y: size.height / 1.3
23           });
24           this.Menu.addChild(this.MenuItem1);
25
26           //Menu item with image
27           this.MenuItem2 = new cc.MenuItemImage(res.MenuItemImage_
             Normal,res.MenuI\
28       temImage_Selected,null,'onMenuClicked',this);
29           this.MenuItem2.attr({
30               x: size.width / 2,
31               y: size.height / 1.8
32           });
33           this.Menu.addChild(this.MenuItem2);
34
35           this.addChild(this.Menu);
36           return true;
37       },
38       onMenuClicked:function(){
39
40       }
41   });
```

First, an instance of cc.Menu is created and added to the layer in the last statement:

```
1    this.Menu=new cc.Menu();
2    ......
3    ......
4    this.addChild(this.Menu);
```

After that, all the menu item instances are created and added as children to this. Menu. The first menuitem is created using a cc.Label instance, as shown here:

```
1   var label=new cc.LabelTTF('MenuItem with label',36);
2   this.MenuItem1 = new cc.MenuItemLabel(label,'onMenuClicked',this);
```

This is later positioned and added as child to this.Menu. The second MenuItemImage is created using two images: normal and selected state images. See here:

```
1   this.MenuItem2 = new cc.MenuItemImage(res.MenuItemImage_Normal,res.
    MenuItemImage\
2   _Selected,null,'onMenuClicked',this);
```

Like in the previous example, LayerColor has been added in this layer, so the output will look like Figure 5-2.

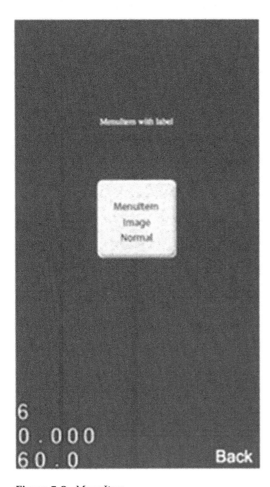

Figure 5-2. *MenuItem*

5.4 Other GUI Elements

Apart from menus and labels, there are other GUI elements that are available in an extension module, such as checkbox and button. In order to use extension classes, we need to add the extension module to our project. In project.json, in the modules property, add 'extension' to the array list:

```
1    "modules" : ["cocos2d","extensions"],
```

These additional user interface elements are available under the parent object ccui. Let's have a look. In the src folder, create a file called otheruidemo.js and copy the following code into it:

```
1    var OtherUIDemoLayer = cc.Layer.extend({
2        sprite:null,
3        ctor:function () {
4            this._super();
5
6            var size = cc.winSize;
7
8            var colorLayer = new cc.LayerColor(cc.color(142,29,42));
9            this.addChild(colorLayer)
10
11           this.uiButton = new ccui.Button(res.ButtonImage,res.
             ButtonImage_Selected\
12   );
13           this.uiButton.attr({
14               x:size.width/2,
15               y:size.height/1.3
16           });
17           this.addChild(this.uiButton);
18
19           this.uiCheckBox = new ccui.CheckBox(res.CheckBox_Normal,res.
             CheckBox_Sel\
20           ected);
21           this.uiCheckBox.attr({
22               x:size.width/2,
23               y:size.height/2
24           });
25           this.addChild(this.uiCheckBox);
26
27           return true;
28       }
29   });
```

57

In this, a button instance has been created with normal and selected images:

```
1   this.uiButton = new ccui.Button(res.ButtonImage,res.ButtonImage_
    Selected);
```

And a checkBox instance has been created, also using normal and selected images:

```
1   this.uiCheckBox = new ccui.CheckBox(res.CheckBox_Normal,res.CheckBox_
    Selected);
```

If you run the preceding layer, the output will look like Figure 5-3.

Figure 5-3. Other GUI elements

CHAPTER 6

■ ■ ■

Fun with Animation

6.1 Introduction

Animation is essential to any good game, as it makes your game cool and visually appealing, and helps you to acquire more users. A visually appealing game markets itself. Take a moment to look at the top-grossing games in Google Play and App Store. Top games use crisp and detail-rich animations to improve the user experience and to engage users. Take a deep breath, as we are going to look at the details of the animation system in Cocos2d-js. Let's begin.

6.2 Actions

Actions are the construct that is used in Cocos2d-js to animate a sprite. Actions change the properties of the sprite over time, and that makes the sprite animate in the way we want. There are several types of actions available with which to apply animations on sprites for all the realtime scenarios. Let's have a look at a simple example:

```
1  var action = cc.moveBy(2, cc.p(size.width - 40, size.height - 40));
2  this.sprite.runAction(action);
```

In this example, the `action` object is created using the `cc.moveBy` function. Any action can be run on sprites using the `runAction` method. This method actually belongs to `cc.Node`, so beyond sprites, we can animate any objects that have `cc.Node` as a parent or topmost parent (i.e., layers, scenes, etc.) Basically, there are two variations in creating actions.

6.2.1 By and To actions

The preceding code is an example of the By variation. Let's have a look at the same example with the To variation:

```
1  var action = cc.moveTo(2, cc.p(size.width - 40, size.height - 40));
2  this.sprite.runAction(action);
```

© Hemanth Kumar 2016

H. Kumar and A. Rahman, *Rapid Game Development Using Cocos2d-JS*,
DOI 10.1007/978-1-4842-2553-0_6

The only difference between By and To actions is that To will animate the target property value to the absolute value, and By will animate the target property value to the relative value (Example: If you have a sprite at location (10,10) and you use the moveBy action to animate with value (5,5), after animation the final position of the sprite would be (15,15); in case of a moveTo action the final position would be (5,5)).

6.3   Available Actions List

The following is the list of available actions that you can apply on any nodes. The listed combinations include By and To variations, which you can try with simple sprite images.

6.3.1   Move

This action is used to animate the x,y position of any node instance:

```
1  var action = cc.moveBy(2, cc.p(size.width - 40, size.height - 40));
2  var action = cc.moveTo(2, cc.p(size.width - 40, size.height - 40));
```

The first parameter is the duration and the second is the target point value.

6.3.2   Jump

This action is used to animate the node's x,y position in a parabolic way such that it looks like it is jumping:

```
1  var action = new cc.JumpBy(2, cc.p(300, 0), 50, 4);
2  var action = new cc.JumpBy(2, 300, 0, 50, 4);
```

The first parameter is the duration, as it is for all actions. The second parameter is a point or number that represents the target value (either x or (x,y)). If it is a point, then the third parameter is considered as height; if it is a number, then the third parameter is considered as a y value. The next two parameters represent height and number of jumps. So in this case (x,y) and height represent the width and height of the parabola.

6.3.3   Rotation

This action is used to animate the rotation of the node by modifying the rotation attribute over time:

```
1  var action = new cc.RotateBy(2, 360);
2  var action = new cc.RotateTo(2, 360);
```

The first parameter is duration and the second parameter is angleX, which rotates around the x axis. The third parameter, angleY, is optional and is used for y rotation in rare cases.

6.3.4 Scale

This action is used to scale animate the node. It uses the scale function of the node to scale the node over the specified duration:

```
1  var action = new cc.ScaleTo(2, 0.5, 2);
2  var action = new cc.ScaleBy(2, 0.5, 2);
```

The first parameter is duration and the second and third are sx,sy, which are scaleX and scaleY values.

6.3.5 Skew

This action is similar to scale, but it uses skewX and skewY values to animate the skew:

```
1  var action = new cc.SkewTo(2, 37.2, -37.2);
2  var action = new cc.SkewBy(2, 37.2, -37.2);
```

Parameters are the same as for scale.

6.3.6 Tint

This action is used to animate the RGB channel of the node; only the By version is available for this action:

```
1  var action = new cc.TintBy(2, -127, -255, -127);
```

The first parameter is duration, and the next three parameters are deltaR, deltaB, and deltaG values.

6.3.7 Bezier

This action is used to move the target through a Bezier curve:

```
1  var bezier = [cc.p(0, windowSize.height / 2), cc.p(300, -windowSize.
   height / 2),\
2  cc.p(300, 100)];
3  var bezierForward = new cc.BezierBy(3, bezier);
4  var bezierTo = new cc.BezierTo(3, bezier);
```

The first parameter is duration and the second is an array that has a list of points that defines the Bezier curve.

6.3.8 Cardinal Spline

This is similar to Bezier. The target will move through a cardinal spline curve. Usually, this action is used when you want to simulate the movement of a sprite over path data, which is a collection of consecutive points. See here:

```
1  var action = cc.cardinalSplineTo(3, array, 0);
2  var action = cc.cardinalSplineTo(3, array, 0);
```

Parameters are the same as for Bezier; however, it has a third parameter that represents tension, or the weight between two points, and calculates the duration of movement from one point to another.

6.4 Easing

By default, all actions that animate the properties of the node over time linearly are called linear interpolation. Such an animation looks straightforward. When you want to add organic effects to your animation, your animation needs an easing function. See Figure 6-1.

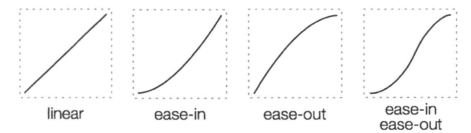

Figure 6-1. Linear and easing

As you can see, the first image is linear, which all actions will use by default. The other three are different easing functions. In Cocos2d-js, there are over 26 types of easing. For all easing functions, the usage is the same. Let's see an example:

```
1  var easing=cc.easeBackIn();
2  //or
3  var easing=new cc.EaseBackIn();
4  action.easing(easing);
```

So simple! In this example, I have used the EaseBackIn class to create the easing object, or you can use a singleton cc.easeBackIn object to run on your action. I prefer the first way. Let's see the list of easing functions available in Cocos2d-js. Remember: usage is the same for all easing functions.

- cc.EaseBackIn
- cc.EaseBackInOut
- cc.EaseBackOut
- cc.EaseBezierAction
- cc.EaseBounce
- cc.EaseBounceIn
- cc.EaseBounceInOut
- cc.EaseBounceOut
- cc.EaseCircleActionIn
- cc.EaseCircleActionInOut
- cc.EaseCircleActionOut
- cc.EaseCubicActionIn
- cc.EaseCubicActionInOut
- cc.EaseCubicActionOut
- cc.EaseElastic
- cc.EaseElasticIn
- cc.EaseElasticInOut
- cc.EaseElasticOut
- cc.EaseExponentialIn
- cc.EaseExponentialInOut
- cc.EaseExponentialOut
- cc.EaseQuadraticActionIn
- cc.EaseQuadraticActionInOut
- cc.EaseQuadraticActionOut
- cc.EaseQuarticActionIn
- cc.EaseQuarticActionInOut
- cc.EaseQuarticActionOut
- cc.EaseQuinticActionIn

- cc.EaseQuinticActionInOut

- cc.EaseQuinticActionOut

- cc.EaseRateAction

- cc.EaseIn

- cc.EaseInOut

- cc.EaseOut

- cc.EaseSineIn

- cc.EaseSineInOut

- cc.EaseSineOut

This list will satisfy all your easing needs. All the easing is derived from cc.ActionEase, which is the base class.

6.5 Sequence

Say, for example, I have two or more actions that need to be performed on a node one after the other. Sequence will help us to do that. Let's see an example:

```
1  var seq = new cc.Sequence([action1,action2]);
2  this.sprite.runAction(seq);
```

cc.Sequence accepts two parameter types: one is an array of actions, and the other one will be discussed later in this section. It can be run using the runAction function of the node, just like any other action.

6.5.1 Reversing Sequence

Once a sequence object is created, it can be reversed and run on any node, as follows:

```
1  this.sprite.runAction(seq.reverse());
```

The reverse function will reverse the actions in sequence and will return a new instance of sequence.

6.5.2 Repeating Sequence

Once a sequence object is created, we can repeat the action a finite number of times, or we can repeat it infinitely. See here:

```
1  //Repeat sequence 5 times
2  this.sprite.runAction(seq.repeat(5));
3
```

```
4   //Repeat sequence forever
5   this.sprite.runAction(seq.repeatForever());
```

The repeat and repeatForever functions of sequence are used for this purpose.

6.5.3   Action End Callback

It is possible in a sequence object to attach an end callback function for each action. Let's see an example:

```
1   var seq=new cc.Sequence(action1,cc.callFunc(function(){/*action1 end
    callback*/}\
2   ,this),
3   action2,cc.callFunc(function(){/*action2 end callback*/}\
4   ,this));
```

As discussed earlier, Sequence accepts two parameter types. One is an array of actions, and the other is a series of actions and their action end callback, like just seen.

6.6   Spawn

There are certain scenarios where you want to execute two or more actions simultaneously on a node. cc.Spawn is used for this purpose:

```
1   var spaw=new cc.Spawn([action1,action2]);
2   this.sprite.runAction(spaw);
```

As you can see, the syntax is similar to Sequence. It accepts an array of actions to be executed simultaneously. Be cautious when you execute multiple actions at the same time, as it may produce a weird effect if not used properly.

6.7   Stopping an Action

Every action can be stopped while it is running. The stopAction function of the node object is used for this purpose:

```
1   sprite.stopAction(action);
```

This stops the action immediately regardless of its state. You can use this for user actions or any dynamic triggers that require actions to be stopped immediately.

6.8   Sprite Frame Animation

In Chapter 3, we saw how sprite frame animation can be done using sprite sheets. That chapter was more focused on sprites, while this section will provide a detailed explanation of it from the animation side. Each and every image part in a sprite can be classified using SpriteFrame with rect coordinates. The cc.Animation class can be used to perform a sprite frame animation sequence on a sprite. Let's see an example:

```
1   var animation = new cc.Animation(spriteFrames, 0.08);
2   this.sprite.runAction(cc.animate(animation).repeatForever()); //or new
    cc.Animat\
3   ion(..) patten can be used.
```

The first parameter is an array of cc.SpriteFrame instances, and the second is the delay. Like the Action class, this also has repeat and repeatForever functions.

6.9   Schedulers and Update

In Cocos2d-js, there is an update loop, which is a main run loop; every cc.Node is capable of receiving update notifications, but the node has to subscribe to it. This subscribe mechanism is implemented with performance considerations in mind.

In the cc.Node, in the ctor, the following method needs to be called:

```
1   this.scheduleUpdate();
```

Once this is done, you can define a method called update:

```
1   update:function(dt) {
2
3   }
```

Let's perform an animation using update. First, create a layer and demo scenes as mentioned in earlier examples, then add a sprite to the scene:

```
1   this.sprite = new cc.Sprite(res.Sprite_Image);
2   this.sprite.attr({
3       x: size.width / 2,
4       y: size.height / 2
5   });
6   this.addChild(this.sprite, 0);
```

We are going to animate the sprite from left to right in a ping-pong fashion. For that we need to have a seed value:

```
1   this.seed=10;
```

Let's define our update method and animate the sprite:

```
1  update:function(dt) {
2    if(this.sprite.getPositionX()>cc.winSize.width){
3      this.seed=-10;
4    } else if(this.sprite.getPositionX()<0) {
5      this.seed=10;
6    }
7    this.sprite.setPositionX(this.sprite.getPositionX()+this.seed);
8  }
```

By now the whole code should look like the following:

```
1   var SchedulersLayer = BaseSampleLayer.extend({
2       sprite:null,
3       ctor:function () {
4
5           this._super();
6
7           var size = cc.winSize;
8
9           this.sprite = new cc.Sprite(res.Sprite_Image);
10          this.sprite.attr({
11              x: size.width / 2,
12              y: size.height / 2
13          });
14          this.seed=10;
15          this.addChild(this.sprite, 0);
16          this.scheduleUpdate();
17
18      },
19      update:function(dt) {
20        if(this.sprite.getPositionX()>cc.winSize.width){
21          this.seed=-10;
22        } else if(this.sprite.getPositionX()<0) {
23          this.seed=10;
24        }
25        this.sprite.setPositionX(this.sprite.getPositionX()+this.seed);
26      }
27  });
```

The output should look like a sprite moving left to right and vice versa in a repeated way. See Figure 6-2.

Figure 6-2. *Schedulers and update*

CHAPTER 7

Adding Physics to Your Game

7.1 Introduction

In physics-based games, simulating the physics of the real world is very important. There are a variety of physics engines available today. The most popular one for Cocos2d-js is Chipmunk physics. This was originally written in C and later was ported to various platforms. Even though you can use other game engines with Cocos2d-js, the Chipmunk engine is highly recommended. It is the native physics engine for Cocos2d-x.

7.2 Chipmunk Overview

Physics is all about altering sprites' x,y position and rotation in the right manner such that it will look like a physics simulation. There is a clear separation between your game world and the physics space. See Figure 7-1.

© Hemanth Kumar 2016

H. Kumar and A. Rahman, *Rapid Game Development Using Cocos2d-JS*,
DOI 10.1007/978-1-4842-2553-0_7

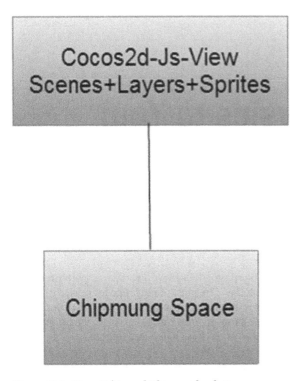

Figure 7-1. *Cocos2d-js and Chipmunk relation*

All the physics bodies and their behavior are defined in the Chipmunk space, and sprites from Cocos2d-js layers are mapped to those bodies. The physics simulation will happen within the Chipmunk space, based on relation mapping with the appropriate sprites. Chipmunk will update the x,y and rotation of those sprites based on the body in the physics space. Let's see the basics in Figure 7-2.

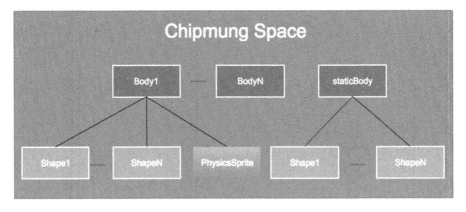

Figure 7-2. *Chipmunk overview*

Physics simulation happens inside the Chipmunk space, where the physics body gets physical properties set; those bodies will have shapes defined, which can be a box or circle or polygon. Every Chipmunk space will have a default staticBody as its child, and shapes added to it will not be affected by physical properties and will be static objects like walls or obstacles, etc. All the bodies will be associated with PhysicsSprite, which has your sprite image, and this sprite's location and rotation will be determined by the physics body associated with it. In the upcoming example, we are going to create a Chipmunk space, add walls to the four boundaries, and add two bodies, a box and a circle, to the space. Then, we are going to watch the simulation.

7.3   Chipmunk Space

The first thing you have to do is include the Chipmunk module in your project.json file:

```
1    "modules" : ["cocos2d",....,"chipmunk"]
```

Let's see how this space can be created:

```
1    initPhysics:function() {
2          //initiate space
3          this.space = new cp.Space();
4
5          //setup the Gravity
6          this.space.gravity = cp.v(0, -800); //Earth gravity
7          this.space.iterations = 30;
8          this.space.sleepTimeThreshold = Infinity;
9          this.space.collisionSlop = Infinity;
10   }
```

This initPhysics function will be placed inside the layer object; that is, initPhysics will be one of the properties of layer object. The cp.Space class is used to create the space, and gravity, iterations, sleepTimeThreshold, and collisionSlop are set to the appropriate values.

```
1    update:function (dt) {
2          this.space.step(dt);
3    },
```

Physics simulation is driven by the step method, which is constantly triggered in the update cycle of layer.

7.4 Chipmunk Body

A physical object is defined by a body; the body has a shape and the sprite's data associated with it. Let's add a circle and box to the created Chipmunk space:

```
1    addPhysicsCircle: function() {
2        var width=50,height=50,mass=1;
3
4        this.phBodyCircle = this.space.addBody(new cp.Body(mass,
         cp.momentForCircle(\
5    mass,0,width*0.5,cc.p(0,0))));
6        this.phBodyCircle.setPos(cc.p(cc.winSize.width * 0.5, cc.winSize.
         height * 0.\
7        3));
8
9        //#4
10       var phShape = this.space.addShape(new cp.CircleShape(this.
         phBodyCircle, widt\
11   h, cc.p(0, 0)));
12       phShape.setFriction(0);
13       phShape.setElasticity(1);
14       phShape.setCollisionType(0);
15   },
16
17   addPhysicsBox: function() {
18       var width=50,height=50,mass=1;
19       this.phBodyBox = this.space.addBody(new cp.Body(mass,
         cp.momentForBox(mass, \
20       width,height)));
21       this.phBodyBox.setPos(cc.p(cc.winSize.width * 0.5, cc.winSize.
         height * 0.1));
22
23       //#4
24       var phShape = this.space.addShape(new cp.BoxShape(this.phBodyBox,
         width, hei\
25       ght));
26       phShape.setFriction(0);
27       phShape.setElasticity(1);
28       phShape.setCollisionType(1);
29   }
```

As you can see, the circle and box bodies are created using `cp.Body` with `mass` and momentum objects, and the shape is defined for each using `cp.CircleShape` and `cp.BoxShape`. This actually serves an important part in physics simulations, and collision-based physical movement is based on these shape objects.

7.5   Chipmunk StaticBody

Chipmunk space will have a single static body. Usually, this staticBody is used to define the physical boundaries and static shapes, such as walls.

```
1   addWallsAndGround: function() {
2           var leftWall = new cp.SegmentShape(this.space.staticBody, new
            cp.v(0, 0),\
3     new cp.v(0, 1000000), WALLS_WIDTH);
4           leftWall.setElasticity(WALLS_ELASTICITY);
5           leftWall.setFriction(WALLS_FRICTION);
6           this.space.addStaticShape(leftWall);
7
8           var rightWall = new cp.SegmentShape(this.space.staticBody, new
            cp.v(cc.wi\
9    nSize.width, 1000000), new cp.v(cc.winSize.width, 0), WALLS_WIDTH);
10          rightWall.setElasticity(WALLS_ELASTICITY);
11          rightWall.setFriction(WALLS_FRICTION);
12          this.space.addStaticShape(rightWall);
13
14          var bottomWall = new cp.SegmentShape(this.space.staticBody, new
            cp.v(0, 0\
15   ), new cp.v(cc.winSize.width, 0), WALLS_WIDTH);
16          bottomWall.setElasticity(WALLS_ELASTICITY);
17          bottomWall.setFriction(WALLS_FRICTION);
18          this.space.addStaticShape(bottomWall);
19
20          var upperWall = new cp.SegmentShape(this.space.staticBody, new
            cp.v(0, cc\
21   .winSize.height), new cp.v(cc.winSize.width, cc.winSize.height), WALLS_
     WIDTH);
22          upperWall.setElasticity(WALLS_ELASTICITY);
23          upperWall.setFriction(WALLS_FRICTION);
24          this.space.addStaticShape(upperWall);
25   }
```

For creating boundaries, Chipmunk has cp.SegmentShape, which is used to create top, bottom, left, and right walls that are added to the default static body in space so that gravity and other forces won't affect this shape.

7.6   Physics Debug Node

A physics body consists of shapes that have polygon data. You have to attach a
PhysicsSprite to the body in order to see the physics body in action; without that,
there is an object called PhysicsDebugNode that you need to add to the layer in order to
see the polygons without sprites. In the preceding example for box and circle shapes,
PhysicsSprite is not attached, so we are going to rely on PhysicsDebugNode:

```
1    setupDebugNode : function()
2    {
3             this._debugNode = new cc.PhysicsDebugNode(this.space);
4             this.addChild( this._debugNode );
5    }
```

Now the circle and box polygon data will be visible on screen without adding
PhysicsSprite.

7.7   Collision Detection

Chipmunk has the ability to detect collisions between physical bodies. Every physics
body has to be tagged with setCollisionType so that it will be visible for collision
detection:

```
1    addCollisionCallBack:function(){
2             // 0 and 1 are tag for box and circle
3             this.space.addCollisionHandler(0, 1, function(){
4                 cc.log('Box and Circle colliding !');
5                 return true;
6             }, null, null, null);
7    }
```

As you can see, the addCollisionHandler function, with the tag 0,1 for box and
circle, has been used to detect any collision between the two objects.

7.8   Putting It All Together

Finally, it is time to put it all together. In the layer constructor, include the following code:

```
1    this.initPhysics();
2    this.setupDebugNode();
3    this.addWallsAndGround();
4    this.addPhysicsCircle();
5    this.addPhysicsBox();
6    this.addCollisionCallBack();
7    this.scheduleUpdate();
```

All the functions except scheduleUpdate have been defined already. The scheduleUpdate function is a node function that enables the node to include its update method for a draw cycle trigger. Finally, you will see something like the following:

```
1    var g_groundHeight = 57;
2    var g_runnerStartX = 80;
3
4    var WALLS_WIDTH = 5;
5    var WALLS_ELASTICITY = 1;
6    var WALLS_FRICTION = 1;
7
8    var ChipmungDemoLayer = BaseSampleLayer.extend({
9        sprite:null,
10       ctor:function () {
11           this._super();
12           this.initPhysics();
13           this.setupDebugNode();
14           this.addWallsAndGround();
15           this.addPhysicsCircle();
16           this.addPhysicsBox();
17           this.addCollisionCallBack();
18
19           this.scheduleUpdate();
20           return true;
21       },
22       initPhysics:function() {
23
24           //initiate space
25           this.space = new cp.Space();
26
27           //setup the Gravity
28           this.space.gravity = cp.v(0, -800); //Earth gravity
29           this.space.iterations = 30;
30           this.space.sleepTimeThreshold = Infinity;
31           this.space.collisionSlop = Infinity;
32       },
33       addCollisionCallBack:function(){
34           // 0 and 1 are tag for box and circle
35           this.space.addCollisionHandler(0, 1, function(){
36               cc.log('Box and Circle collaiding !');
37               return true;
38           }, null, null, null);
39       },
40       update:function (dt) {
41           this.space.step(dt);
42       },
```

```
43          addWallsAndGround: function() {
44              var leftWall = new cp.SegmentShape(this.space.staticBody, new
                cp.v(0\
45  , 0), new cp.v(0, 1000000), WALLS_WIDTH);
46                  leftWall.setElasticity(WALLS_ELASTICITY);
47                  leftWall.setFriction(WALLS_FRICTION);
48                  this.space.addStaticShape(leftWall);
49
50                  var rightWall = new cp.SegmentShape(this.space.staticBody,
                    new cp.v(\
51  cc.winSize.width, 1000000), new cp.v(cc.winSize.width, 0), WALLS_
    WIDTH);
52                  rightWall.setElasticity(WALLS_ELASTICITY);
53                  rightWall.setFriction(WALLS_FRICTION);
54                  this.space.addStaticShape(rightWall);
55
56                  var bottomWall = new cp.SegmentShape(this.space.
                    staticBody, new cp.v\
57  (0, 0), new cp.v(cc.winSize.width, 0), WALLS_WIDTH);
58                  bottomWall.setElasticity(WALLS_ELASTICITY);
59                  bottomWall.setFriction(WALLS_FRICTION);
60                  this.space.addStaticShape(bottomWall);
61
62                  var upperWall = new cp.SegmentShape(this.space.staticBody,
                    new cp.v(\
63  0, cc.winSize.height), new cp.v(cc.winSize.width, cc.winSize.height),
    WALLS_WIDT\
64  H);
65                  upperWall.setElasticity(WALLS_ELASTICITY);
66                  upperWall.setFriction(WALLS_FRICTION);
67                  this.space.addStaticShape(upperWall);
68
69          },
70          setupDebugNode : function()
71          {
72              this._debugNode = new cc.PhysicsDebugNode(this.space);
73              this.addChild( this._debugNode );
74          },
75          addPhysicsCircle: function() {
76            var width=50,height=50,mass=1;
77
78            this.phBodyCircle = this.space.addBody(new cp.Body(mass,
              cp.momentForC\
79            ircle(mass,0,width*0.5,cc.p(0,0))));
80            this.phBodyCircle.setPos(cc.p(cc.winSize.width * 0.5,
              cc.winSize.heigh\
81  t * 0.3));
82
```

```
83          //#4
84          var phShape = this.space.addShape(new cp.CircleShape(this.
            phBodyCircle\
85    , width, cc.p(0, 0)));
86              phShape.setFriction(0);
87              phShape.setElasticity(1);
88              phShape.setCollisionType(0);
89          },
90
91          addPhysicsBox: function() {
92            var width=50,height=50,mass=1;
93            this.phBodyBox = this.space.addBody(new cp.Body(mass,
              cp.momentForBox(\
94    mass, width,height)));
95              this.phBodyBox.setPos(cc.p(cc.winSize.width * 0.5,
              cc.winSize.height *\
96            0.1));
97
98            //#4
99            var phShape = this.space.addShape(new cp.BoxShape(this.
              phBodyBox, widt\
100           h, height));
101             phShape.setFriction(0);
102             phShape.setElasticity(1);
103             phShape.setCollisionType(1);
104         }
105   });
```

And the output should look like Figure 7-3.

Figure 7-3. Physics demo

7.9   Joints

Joints are nothing but joining two physics bodies with anchor points or relating them with some physical behaviors. In the real world, things we encounter–from your phone to your car–are a collection of different pieces of objects joined together with joints and nails. The same is true for chipmunk bodies. There are different types of joints available in Chipmunk, as follows:

- Pin Joint
- Slide Joint
- Pivot Joint
- Groove Joint
- Damped Spring
- Damped Rotary Spring

- Rotary Limit Joint

- Simple Motor

- Gear Joint

- Ratchet Joint

We are going to look into all the preceding joints with examples, but before we do there are some common functions that we are going to use in all of these examples. Let's have a look:

```
1   addBottomWall: function() {
2     var bottomWall = new cp.SegmentShape(this.space.staticBody, new
      cp.v(0, 0),
3     new cp.v(cc.winSize.width, 0), 5);
4     bottomWall.setElasticity(1);
5     bottomWall.setFriction(1);
6     this.space.addStaticShape(bottomWall);
7   }
```

This function adds the bottom wall to the Chipmunk space so that the physics body won't fall below the screen. This wall is made up of SegmentShape and is added to the static body in the Chipmunk space.

```
1    addPhysicsCircle: function(pos) {
2      var width=50,height=50,mass=1;
3
4      var phBodyCircle = this.space.addBody(new cp.Body(mass,
5      cp.momentForCircle(mass,0,width*0.5,cc.p(0,0))));
6      phBodyCircle.setPos(pos);
7
8      var phShape = this.space.addShape(new cp.CircleShape(phBodyCircle,
       width, \
9      cc.p(0, 0)));
10     phShape.setFriction(0);
11     phShape.setElasticity(1);
12     phShape.setCollisionType(0);
13
14     return phBodyCircle;
15   }
```

The preceding function adds a circle body to the space and returns that physics body so that we can add constrains to it.

```
1    addPhysicsBox: function(pos) {
2      var width=50,height=50,mass=1;
3      var phBodyBox = this.space.addBody(new cp.Body(mass,
4      cp.momentForBox(mass, width,height)));
5      phBodyBox.setPos(pos);
```

```
 6
 7    var phShape = this.space.addShape(new cp.BoxShape(phBodyBox, width,
      height\
 8  ));
 9    phShape.setFriction(0);
10    phShape.setElasticity(1);
11    phShape.setCollisionType(1);
12
13    return phBodyBox;
14  }
```

This function adds a box body to the space and returns that physics body to use it for applying constrains.

```
1  this.space.addConstraint(constrainObj);
```

Through the constraint, we establish physical relations between two bodies in the space. We will be using this for all the listed constraints. We assume you will create a separate layer for each joint example; however, we included the full source with the layer at the end of every joint example. Let's have a look at joints.

7.9.1   Pin Joint

A pin joint is nothing but connecting two physics bodies with their respective anchor points. For instance, consider two physical bodies, bodyA,bodyB, and anchorA,anchorB are the corresponding anchor points for those bodies; they are given in body space coordinates. The distance between these anchor points is determined when the joint is created and will remain the same throughout the space simulation. For a realworld example, consider a wheel driven by a piston; wheel and piston are connected by a rod, which drives the wheel. The length of the rod remains same.

Let's have a look at an example. First, do the initial setup:

```
1  this.initPhysics();
2  this.setupDebugNode();
3  this.addBottomWall();
```

In Chipmunk space, add two bodies, a box and a circle, using the method explained in the beginning:

```
1  var bodyA = this.addPhysicsCircle(cc.p(cc.winSize.width * 0.25,
2  cc.winSize.height * 0.3));
3
4  var bodyB = this.addPhysicsBox(cc.p(cc.winSize.width * 0.75,
5  cc.winSize.height * 0.3));
```

Then, connect bodyA and bodyB with a pin joint and add it to the constraint:

```
1  var pinJoint = new cp.PinJoint(bodyA, bodyB, cc.p(50,0), cc.p(25,0));
2  this.space.addConstraint(pinJoint);
```

The PinJoint class constructor has four parameters:

- bodyA - first physics body to be connected

- bodyB - second physics body to be connected

- anchorA - point on bodyA

- anchorB - point on bodyB

The full layer source code looks like the following:

```
1   var PinJointLayer = BaseSampleLayer.extend({
2       sprite:null,
3       ctor:function () {
4           this._super();
5           this.initPhysics();
6           this.setupDebugNode();
7           this.addBottomWall();
8
9           var bodyA = this.addPhysicsCircle(cc.p(cc.winSize.width * 0.25,
            cc.win\
10  Size.height * 0.3));
11          var bodyB = this.addPhysicsBox(cc.p(cc.winSize.width * 0.75,
            cc.winSiz\
12  e.height * 0.3));
13
14          var pinJoint = new cp.PinJoint(bodyA, bodyB, cc.p(50,0),
            cc.p(25,0));
15          this.space.addConstraint(pinJoint);
16
17          this.scheduleUpdate();
18          return true;
19      },
20      initPhysics:function() {
21          //initiate space
22          this.space = new cp.Space();
23          //set up the Gravity
24          this.space.gravity = cp.v(0, -800); //Earth gravity
25          this.space.iterations = 30;
26          this.space.sleepTimeThreshold = Infinity;
27          this.space.collisionSlop = Infinity;
28      },
29
```

```
30        update:function (dt) {
31          this.space.step(dt);
32        },
33        addBottomWall: function() {
34          var bottomWall = new cp.SegmentShape(this.space.staticBody,
35            new cp.v(0, 0), new cp.v(cc.winSize.width, 0), 5);
36          bottomWall.setElasticity(1);
37          bottomWall.setFriction(1);
38          this.space.addStaticShape(bottomWall);
39        },
40        setupDebugNode : function()
41        {
42          this._debugNode = new cc.PhysicsDebugNode(this.space);
43          this.addChild( this._debugNode );
44        },
45        addPhysicsCircle: function(pos) {
46          var width=50,height=50,mass=1;
47
48          var phBodyCircle = this.space.addBody(new cp.Body(mass,
49            cp.momentForCircle(mass,0,width*0.5,cc.p(0,0))));
50          phBodyCircle.setPos(pos);
51
52          var phShape = this.space.addShape(new
            cp.CircleShape(phBodyCircle, wid\
53          th, cc.p(0, 0)));
54          phShape.setFriction(0);
55          phShape.setElasticity(1);
56          phShape.setCollisionType(0);
57
58          return phBodyCircle;
59        },
60
61      addPhysicsBox: function(pos) {
62        var width=50,height=50,mass=1;
63        var phBodyBox = this.space.addBody(new cp.Body(mass,
          cp.momentForBox(m\
64  ass, width,height)));
65            phBodyBox.setPos(pos);
66
67            var phShape = this.space.addShape(new cp.BoxShape(phBodyBox,
              width, he\
68            ight));
69            phShape.setFriction(0);
70            phShape.setElasticity(1);
71            phShape.setCollisionType(1);
72
73            return phBodyBox;
74          }
75    });
```

82

And you will see the output shown in Figure 7-4.

Figure 7-4. *Pin joint*

7.9.2   Slide Joint

Similar to a pin joint, two physics bodies can be connected through anchor points with a slide joint. The only difference here is that the distance between anchor points will vary between specified max and min lengths based on the physical simulation. That is, the distance between two anchor points can vary over time but cannot go below the mentioned min length and cannot go above the mentioned max length.

Let's have a look at an example. First, do the initial setup for initiating the Chipmunk space and bottom wall and setting a debug node. In this example, we are going to use a circle and the default static body of Chipmunk, which is a background wall:

```
1    var bodyA = this.addPhysicsCircle(cc.p(cc.winSize.width * 0.5, 0));
2    var bodyB=this.space.staticBody;
```

Then, add a slide joint connecting the static body and circle:

```
1   var slideJoint = new cp.SlideJoint(bodyA, bodyB, cc.p(50,0),
2       cc.p(cc.winSize.width/2,cc.winSize.height), 100, cc.winSize.
        width/2);
3
4   this.space.addConstraint(slideJoint);
```

In addition to a pin joint, we have to specify the min length, max length, and last two parameters. It will look like a ball hanging from the ceiling. Here is the full source code of the layer:

```
1   var SlideJointLayer = BaseSampleLayer.extend({
2       sprite:null,
3       ctor:function () {
4           this._super();
5           this.initPhysics();
6           this.setupDebugNode();
7           this.addBottomWall();
8
9           var bodyA = this.addPhysicsCircle(cc.p(cc.winSize.width * 0.5,
                0));
10          var bodyB=this.space.staticBody;
11
12          var slideJoint = new cp.SlideJoint(bodyA, bodyB, cc.p(50,0),
13          cc.p(cc.winSize.width/2,cc.winSize.height), 100, cc.winSize.
            width/2);
14
15          this.space.addConstraint(slideJoint);
16
17          this.scheduleUpdate();
18          return true;
19      },
20      initPhysics:function() {
21          //initiate space
22          this.space = new cp.Space();
23          //set up the Gravity
24          this.space.gravity = cp.v(0, -800); //Earth gravity
25          this.space.iterations = 30;
26          this.space.sleepTimeThreshold = Infinity;
27          this.space.collisionSlop = Infinity;
28      },
29
```

```
30      update:function (dt) {
31        this.space.step(dt);
32      },
33      addBottomWall: function() {
34        var bottomWall = new cp.SegmentShape(this.space.staticBody,
          new cp.v(0\
35        , 0), new cp.v(cc.winSize.width, 0), 5);
36        bottomWall.setElasticity(1);
37        bottomWall.setFriction(1);
38        this.space.addStaticShape(bottomWall);
39      },
40      setupDebugNode : function()
41      {
42        this._debugNode = new cc.PhysicsDebugNode(this.space);
43        this.addChild( this._debugNode );
44      },
45      addPhysicsCircle: function(pos) {
46        var width=50,height=50,mass=1;
47
48        var phBodyCircle = this.space.addBody(new cp.Body(mass,
          cp.momentForCi\
49        rcle(mass,0,width*0.5,cc.p(0,0))));
50        phBodyCircle.setPos(pos);
51
52        var phShape = this.space.addShape(new
          cp.CircleShape(phBodyCircle, wid\
53        th, cc.p(0, 0)));
54        phShape.setFriction(0);
55        phShape.setElasticity(1);
56        phShape.setCollisionType(0);
57
58        return phBodyCircle;
59      }
60   });
```

And you will see the output shown in Figure 7-5.

Figure 7-5. *Slide joint*

7.9.3   Pivot Joint

In a pivot joint, two physics bodies will be connected using a single anchor point. The position and angle of the two bodies with respect to the anchor point will be determined by the initial positioning of the bodies and anchor point. It is more like two pin joints: one between bodyA's default anchor point and the joint anchor point, and one between bodyB's default anchor point and the joint anchor point. The constraint will be maintained throughout.

First, do the initial setup for the Chipmunk space, then add the circle and box:

```
1   var bodyA = this.addPhysicsCircle(cc.p(cc.winSize.width * 0.25,
2   cc.winSize.height * 0.3));
3
4   var bodyB = this.addPhysicsBox(cc.p(cc.winSize.width * 0.75,
5   cc.winSize.height * 0.3));
```

Now, let's add pivot constraints to these bodies:

```
1   var pivotJoint = new cp.PivotJoint(bodyA, bodyB, cc.p(cc.winSize.width
    * 0.5,
2   cc.winSize.height * 0.5));
3
4   this.space.addConstraint(pivotJoint);
```

Apart from bodyA and bodyB, it has an anchor point as the last parameter. The full code should look like the following:

```
1    var PivotJointLayer = BaseSampleLayer.extend({
2        sprite:null,
3        ctor:function () {
4            this._super();
5            this.initPhysics();
6            this.setupDebugNode();
7            this.addBottomWall();
8
9            var bodyA = this.addPhysicsCircle(cc.p(cc.winSize.width * 0.25,
             cc.win\
10   Size.height * 0.3));
11           var bodyB = this.addPhysicsBox(cc.p(cc.winSize.width * 0.75,
             cc.winSiz\
12           e.height * 0.3));
13
14           var pivotJoint = new cp.PivotJoint(bodyA, bodyB, cc.p(cc.
             winSize.width\
15           * 0.5, cc.winSize.height * 0.5));
16           this.space.addConstraint(pivotJoint);
17
18           this.scheduleUpdate();
19           return true;
20       },
21       initPhysics:function() {
22           //initiate space
23           this.space = new cp.Space();
24           //set up the Gravity
25           this.space.gravity = cp.v(0, -800); //Earth gravity
26           this.space.iterations = 30;
27           this.space.sleepTimeThreshold = Infinity;
28           this.space.collisionSlop = Infinity;
29       },
30
31       update:function (dt) {
32           this.space.step(dt);
33       },
```

```
34      addBottomWall: function() {
35        var bottomWall = new cp.SegmentShape(this.space.staticBody, new
          cp.v(0\
36        , 0), new cp.v(cc.winSize.width, 0), 5);
37        bottomWall.setElasticity(1);
38        bottomWall.setFriction(1);
39        this.space.addStaticShape(bottomWall);
40      },
41      setupDebugNode : function()
42      {
43        this._debugNode = new cc.PhysicsDebugNode(this.space);
44        this.addChild( this._debugNode );
45      },
46      addPhysicsCircle: function(pos) {
47        var width=50,height=50,mass=1;
48
49        var phBodyCircle = this.space.addBody(new cp.Body(mass,
          cp.momentForCi\
50        rcle(mass,0,width*0.5,cc.p(0,0))));
51        phBodyCircle.setPos(pos);
52
53        var phShape = this.space.addShape(new
          cp.CircleShape(phBodyCircle, wid\
54        th, cc.p(0, 0)));
55        phShape.setFriction(0);
56        phShape.setElasticity(1);
57        phShape.setCollisionType(0);
58
59        return phBodyCircle;
60      },
61
62      addPhysicsBox: function(pos) {
63        var width=50,height=50,mass=1;
64        var phBodyBox = this.space.addBody(new cp.Body(mass,
          cp.momentForBox(m\
65        ass, width,height)));
66         phBodyBox.setPos(pos);
67
68         var phShape = this.space.addShape(new cp.BoxShape(phBodyBox,
          width, he\
69         ight));
70        phShape.setFriction(0);
71        phShape.setElasticity(1);
72        phShape.setCollisionType(1);
73
74        return phBodyBox;
75      }
76  });
```

And the output will look like Figure 7-6.

Figure 7-6. *Pivot joint*

7.9.4   Groove Joint

In a groove joint, there will be two groove points, groove_a and groove_b, in the world coordinates. There is also bodyB, which is connected though its anchor point via groove joint slides between groove_a and groove_b. The positions of groove_a and groove_b vary based on the position and rotation of bodyA.

First, do the initial chipmunk setup. To visualize this in a better way, we are going to add a circle and establish a slide joint between the circle and static body:

```
1  var bodyA = this.addPhysicsCircle(cc.p(cc.winSize.width * 0.25,
   cc.winSize.h\
2  eight * 0.3));
3  var bodyB = this.addPhysicsBox(cc.p(cc.winSize.width * 0.75, cc.winSize.
   heig\
4  ht * 0.3));
5  var bodyC=this.space.staticBody;
6
```

```
7   var slideJoint = new cp.SlideJoint(bodyA, bodyC, cc.p(-50,0),
8   cc.p(cc.winSize.width/2,cc.winSize.height), 100, cc.winSize.width/2);
9   this.space.addConstraint(slideJoint);
```

Now, we are going to add a groove joint and link bodyA and bodyB:

```
1   var x=cc.winSize.width/2;
2
3   var grooveJoint = new cp.GrooveJoint(bodyA, bodyB, cc.p(x,0),
4   cc.p(x,50), cc.p(25,0));
5
6   this.space.addConstraint(grooveJoint);
```

Parameters are bodyA, bodyB, groove_a, groove_b, and anchor.
Here is the full source code of the layer:

```
1    var GrooveJointLayer = BaseSampleLayer.extend({
2        sprite:null,
3        ctor:function () {
4            this._super();
5            this.initPhysics();
6            this.setupDebugNode();
7            this.addBottomWall();
8
9            var bodyA = this.addPhysicsCircle(cc.p(cc.winSize.width * 0.25,
             cc.win\
10           Size.height * 0.3));
11           var bodyB = this.addPhysicsBox(cc.p(cc.winSize.width * 0.75,
             cc.winSiz\
12           e.height * 0.3));
13           var bodyC=this.space.staticBody;
14
15           var slideJoint = new cp.SlideJoint(bodyA, bodyC, cc.p(-50,0),
16           cc.p(cc.winSize.width/2,cc.winSize.height), 100, cc.winSize.
             width/2);
17           this.space.addConstraint(slideJoint);
18
19           var x=cc.winSize.width/2;
20
21           var grooveJoint = new cp.GrooveJoint(bodyA, bodyB, cc.p(x,0),
             cc.p(x,5\
22           0), cc.p(25,0));
23           this.space.addConstraint(grooveJoint);
24
25           this.scheduleUpdate();
26           return true;
27        },
```

```
28      initPhysics:function() {
29        //initiate space
30        this.space = new cp.Space();
31        //set up the Gravity
32        this.space.gravity = cp.v(0, -800); //Earth gravity
33        this.space.iterations = 30;
34        this.space.sleepTimeThreshold = Infinity;
35        this.space.collisionSlop = Infinity;
36      },
37
38      update:function (dt) {
39        this.space.step(dt);
40      },
41      addBottomWall: function() {
42        var bottomWall = new cp.SegmentShape(this.space.staticBody, new
          cp.v(0\
43    , 0), new cp.v(cc.winSize.width, 0), 5);
44        bottomWall.setElasticity(1);
45        bottomWall.setFriction(1);
46        this.space.addStaticShape(bottomWall);
47      },
48      setupDebugNode : function()
49      {
50        this._debugNode = new cc.PhysicsDebugNode(this.space);
51        this.addChild( this._debugNode );
52      },
53      addPhysicsCircle: function(pos) {
54        var width=50,height=50,mass=1;
55
56        var phBodyCircle = this.space.addBody(new cp.Body(mass,
          cp.momentForCi\
57    rcle(mass,0,width*0.5,cc.p(0,0))));
58        phBodyCircle.setPos(pos);
59
60        var phShape = this.space.addShape(new
          cp.CircleShape(phBodyCircle, wid\
61    th, cc.p(0, 0)));
62        phShape.setFriction(0);
63        phShape.setElasticity(1);
64        phShape.setCollisionType(0);
65
66        return phBodyCircle;
67      },
68
69      addPhysicsBox: function(pos) {
70        var width=50,height=50,mass=1;
```

```
71        var phBodyBox = this.space.addBody(new cp.Body(mass,
          cp.momentForBox(m\
72        ass, width,height)));
73        phBodyBox.setPos(pos);
74
75        var phShape = this.space.addShape(new cp.BoxShape(phBodyBox,
          width, he\
76        ight));
77        phShape.setFriction(0);
78        phShape.setElasticity(1);
79        phShape.setCollisionType(1);
80
81        return phBodyBox;
82      }
83   });
```

And you will see the output shown in Figure 7-7.

Figure 7-7. *Groove joint*

7.9.5   Damped Spring

In damped spring, bodyA and bodyB will be connected to the two ends of the spring, and we have to provide other parameters that define the behavior of the spring.

First, initialize the Chipmunk space. Like in the previous example, we are going to add a circle and establish a slide joint to the static body for better visualization. See here:

```
1  var bodyA = this.addPhysicsCircle(cc.p(cc.winSize.width * 0.25,
   cc.winSize.h\
2  eight * 0.3));
3  var bodyB = this.addPhysicsBox(cc.p(cc.winSize.width * 0.75, cc.winSize.
   heig\
4  ht * 0.3));
5  var bodyC=this.space.staticBody;
6
7  var slideJoint = new cp.SlideJoint(bodyA, bodyC, cc.p(-50,0),
8  cc.p(cc.winSize.width/2,cc.winSize.height), 100, cc.winSize.width/2);
9  this.space.addConstraint(slideJoint);
```

Then, add a damped spring between bodyA and bodyB:

```
1  var dampedSpring = new cp.DampedSpring(bodyA, bodyB, cc.p(50,0),
2  cc.p(25,0), 25, 5, 0.6);
3
4  this.space.addConstraint(dampedSpring);
```

After bodyA and bodyB, there are five parameters:

- anchorA - anchor point for bodyA

- anchorB - anchor point for bodyB

- resLength - normal length the spring wants to be

- stiffness - the spring constant (refer to Young's modulus)

- damping - indicates the softness of damping

Here is the full source code of the layer:

```
1  var DampedSpringLayer = BaseSampleLayer.extend({
2      sprite:null,
3      ctor:function () {
4          this._super();
5          this.initPhysics();
6          this.setupDebugNode();
7          this.addBottomWall();
8
```

```
 9          var bodyA = this.addPhysicsCircle(cc.p(cc.winSize.width * 0.25,
            cc.win\
10   Size.height * 0.3));
11          var bodyB = this.addPhysicsBox(cc.p(cc.winSize.width * 0.75,
            cc.winSiz\
12          e.height * 0.3));
13          var bodyC=this.space.staticBody;
14
15          var slideJoint = new cp.SlideJoint(bodyA, bodyC, cc.p(-50,0),
16   cc.p(cc.winSize.width/2,cc.winSize.height), 100, cc.winSize.width/2);
17          this.space.addConstraint(slideJoint);
18
19          var dampedSpring = new cp.DampedSpring(bodyA, bodyB,
            cc.p(50,0), cc.p(\
20          25,0), 25, 5, 0.6);
21          this.space.addConstraint(dampedSpring);
22
23          this.scheduleUpdate();
24          return true;
25        },
26      initPhysics:function() {
27        //initiate space
28        this.space = new cp.Space();
29        //set up the Gravity
30        this.space.gravity = cp.v(0, -800); //Earth gravity
31        this.space.iterations = 30;
32        this.space.sleepTimeThreshold = Infinity;
33        this.space.collisionSlop = Infinity;
34        },
35
36      update:function (dt) {
37        this.space.step(dt);
38        },
39      addBottomWall: function() {
40        var bottomWall = new cp.SegmentShape(this.space.staticBody, new
          cp.v(0\
41          , 0), new cp.v(cc.winSize.width, 0), 5);
42        bottomWall.setElasticity(1);
43        bottomWall.setFriction(1);
44        this.space.addStaticShape(bottomWall);
45        },
46       setupDebugNode : function()
47       {
48         this._debugNode = new cc.PhysicsDebugNode(this.space);
49         this.addChild( this._debugNode );
50        },
```

```
51      addPhysicsCircle: function(pos) {
52        var width=50,height=50,mass=1;
53
54        var phBodyCircle = this.space.addBody(new cp.Body(mass,
          cp.momentForCi\
55        rcle(mass,0,width*0.5,cc.p(0,0))));
56        phBodyCircle.setPos(pos);
57
58        var phShape = this.space.addShape(new
          cp.CircleShape(phBodyCircle, wid\
59        th, cc.p(0, 0)));
60        phShape.setFriction(0);
61        phShape.setElasticity(1);
62        phShape.setCollisionType(0);
63
64        return phBodyCircle;
65      },
66
67      addPhysicsBox: function(pos) {
68        var width=50,height=50,mass=1;
69        var phBodyBox = this.space.addBody(new cp.Body(mass,
          cp.momentForBox(m\
70        ass, width,height)));
71        phBodyBox.setPos(pos);
72
73        var phShape = this.space.addShape(new cp.BoxShape(phBodyBox,
          width, he\
74        ight));
75        phShape.setFriction(0);
76        phShape.setElasticity(1);
77        phShape.setCollisionType(1);
78
79        return phBodyBox;
80      }
81    });
```

And the output will look like Figure 7-8.

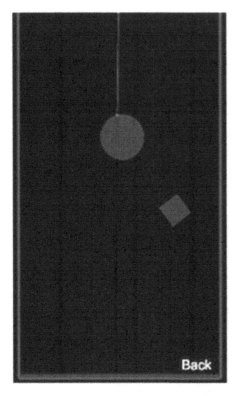

Figure 7-8. *Damped spring*

7.9.6   Damped Rotary Spring

This is similar to the damped spring, the only difference being that it works in an angular fashion. Instead of connecting two bodies with anchor points, two bodies will be linked though a relative angle at which the bodies want to be; stiffness and damping determine the position of the bodies at any time.

Like in previous examples, set up the Chipmunk space, add a circle, and establish a slide joint between the circle and static body, then add a damped rotary spring:

```
1   var dampedRotarySpring = new cp.DampedRotarySpring(bodyA, bodyB, 0, 25,
    0.6);
2   this.space.addConstraint(dampedRotarySpring);
```

Here, the parameters are bodyA, bodyB, restAngle, stiffness, and damping; refer to the previous example for parameter descriptions.

Here is the full source code of the layer:

```
1    var DampedRotarySpringLayer = BaseSampleLayer.extend({
2        sprite:null,
3        ctor:function () {
4            this._super();
5            this.initPhysics();
6            this.setupDebugNode();
7            this.addBottomWall();
8
9            var bodyA = this.addPhysicsCircle(cc.p(cc.winSize.width * 0.25,
             cc.win\
10           Size.height * 0.3));
11           var bodyB = this.addPhysicsBox(cc.p(cc.winSize.width * 0.75,
             cc.winSiz\
12           e.height * 0.3));
13           var bodyC=this.space.staticBody;
14
15           var slideJoint = new cp.SlideJoint(bodyA, bodyC, cc.p(-50,0),
16           cc.p(cc.winSize.width/2,cc.winSize.height), 100, cc.winSize.
             width/2);
17           this.space.addConstraint(slideJoint);
18
19           var dampedRotarySpring = new cp.DampedRotarySpring(bodyA, bodyB,
             0, 25\
20           , 0.6);
21           this.space.addConstraint(dampedRotarySpring);
22
23           this.scheduleUpdate();
24           return true;
25       },
26       initPhysics:function() {
27           //initiate space
28           this.space = new cp.Space();
29           //set up the Gravity
30           this.space.gravity = cp.v(0, -800); //Earth gravity
31           this.space.iterations = 30;
32           this.space.sleepTimeThreshold = Infinity;
33           this.space.collisionSlop = Infinity;
34       },
35
36       update:function (dt) {
37           this.space.step(dt);
38       },
39       addBottomWall: function() {
40           var bottomWall = new cp.SegmentShape(this.space.staticBody, new
             cp.v(0\
41   , 0), new cp.v(cc.winSize.width, 0), 5);
42           bottomWall.setElasticity(1);
```

```
43        bottomWall.setFriction(1);
44        this.space.addStaticShape(bottomWall);
45      },
46      setupDebugNode : function()
47      {
48        this._debugNode = new cc.PhysicsDebugNode(this.space);
49        this.addChild( this._debugNode );
50      },
51      addPhysicsCircle: function(pos) {
52        var width=50,height=50,mass=1;
53
54        var phBodyCircle = this.space.addBody(new cp.Body(mass,
          cp.momentForCi\
55        rcle(mass,0,width*0.5,cc.p(0,0))));
56        phBodyCircle.setPos(pos);
57
58        var phShape = this.space.addShape(new
          cp.CircleShape(phBodyCircle, wid\
59        th, cc.p(0, 0)));
60        phShape.setFriction(0);
61        phShape.setElasticity(1);
62        phShape.setCollisionType(0);
63
64        return phBodyCircle;
65      },
66
67      addPhysicsBox: function(pos) {
68        var width=50,height=50,mass=1;
69        var phBodyBox = this.space.addBody(new cp.Body(mass,
          cp.momentForBox(m\
70        ass, width,height)));
71        phBodyBox.setPos(pos);
72
73        var phShape = this.space.addShape(new cp.BoxShape(phBodyBox,
          width, he\
74        ight));
75        phShape.setFriction(0);
76        phShape.setElasticity(1);
77        phShape.setCollisionType(1);
78
79        return phBodyBox;
80      }
81  });
```

And the output should look like Figure 7-9.

Figure 7-9. *Damped rotary spring*

7.9.7 Rotary Limit Joint

A rotary limit joint constrains the relative rotation of two bodies, provided min and max angular limits. If bodyA and bodyB are linked with a rotary limit joint with min and max angles, the relative rotation of the two bodies will be such that the rotation angle won't go below the min angle and won't exceed the max angle for both bodies.

Like in previous examples, initialize the Chipmunk space and add a circle, then link it with the static body through a slide joint. Now, apply a rotary link between bodyA and bodyB:

```
1  var rotaryLimitJoint = new cp.RotaryLimitJoint(bodyA, bodyB, -Math.PI/2,
   Mat\
2  h.PI/2);
3  this.space.addConstraint(rotaryLimitJoint);
```

After bodyA and bodyB, the min and max angles are provided so that the relative rotation of both bodies will be in this range.

The following is the full source code of the layer:

```
1   var RotaryLimitJointLayer = BaseSampleLayer.extend({
2       sprite:null,
3       ctor:function () {
4           this._super();
5           this.initPhysics();
6           this.setupDebugNode();
7           this.addBottomWall();
8
9           var bodyA = this.addPhysicsCircle(cc.p(cc.winSize.width * 0.25,
            cc.win\
10  Size.height * 0.3));
11          var bodyB = this.addPhysicsBox(cc.p(cc.winSize.width * 0.75,
            cc.winSiz\
12          e.height * 0.3));
13          var bodyC=this.space.staticBody;
14
15          var rotaryLimitJoint = new cp.RotaryLimitJoint(bodyA, bodyB,
            -Math.PI/\
16          2, Math.PI/2);
17          this.space.addConstraint(rotaryLimitJoint);
18
19          var slideJoint = new cp.SlideJoint(bodyA, bodyC, cc.p(-50,0),
20          cc.p(cc.winSize.width/2,cc.winSize.height), 100, cc.winSize.
            width/2);
21          this.space.addConstraint(slideJoint);
22
23          this.scheduleUpdate();
24          return true;
25      },
26      initPhysics:function() {
27          //initiate space
28          this.space = new cp.Space();
29          //set up the Gravity
30          this.space.gravity = cp.v(0, -800); //Earth gravity
31          this.space.iterations = 30;
32          this.space.sleepTimeThreshold = Infinity;
33          this.space.collisionSlop = Infinity;
34      },
35
36      update:function (dt) {
37          this.space.step(dt);
38      },
```

```
39    addBottomWall: function() {
40        var bottomWall = new cp.SegmentShape(this.space.staticBody, new
          cp.v(0\
41        , 0), new cp.v(cc.winSize.width, 0), 5);
42        bottomWall.setElasticity(1);
43        bottomWall.setFriction(1);
44        this.space.addStaticShape(bottomWall);
45    },
46    setupDebugNode : function()
47    {
48        this._debugNode = new cc.PhysicsDebugNode(this.space);
49        this.addChild( this._debugNode );
50    },
51    addPhysicsCircle: function(pos) {
52        var width=50,height=50,mass=1;
53
54        var phBodyCircle = this.space.addBody(new cp.Body(mass,
          cp.momentForCi\
55 rcle(mass,0,width*0.5,cc.p(0,0))));
56        phBodyCircle.setPos(pos);
57
58        var phShape = this.space.addShape(new cp.CircleShape(phBodyCircle,
          wid\
59 th, cc.p(0, 0)));
60        phShape.setFriction(0);
61        phShape.setElasticity(1);
62        phShape.setCollisionType(0);
63
64        return phBodyCircle;
65    },
66
67    addPhysicsBox: function(pos) {
68        var width=50,height=50,mass=1;
69        var phBodyBox = this.space.addBody(new cp.Body(mass,
          cp.momentForBox(m\
70 ass, width,height)));
71        phBodyBox.setPos(pos);
72
73        var phShape = this.space.addShape(new cp.BoxShape(phBodyBox,
          width, he\
74 ight));
75        phShape.setFriction(0);
76        phShape.setElasticity(1);
77        phShape.setCollisionType(1);
78
79        return phBodyBox;
80    }
81 });
```

The output will be the same as for the damped rotary spring; however, you will find differences in the rotation of the two bodies.

7.9.8   Simple Motor

Simple motor maintains the relative angular velocity of two bodies with the provided rate of angular rotation; that is, when bodyA and bodyB are involved, simple motor maintains the relative rotation of the two bodies with the provided angular velocity.

First, set up the Chipmunk space and add two boxes to the space:

```
1   var bodyA = this.addPhysicsBox(cc.p(cc.winSize.width * 0.25,
2             cc.winSize.height * 0.5));
3
4   var bodyB = this.addPhysicsBox(cc.p(cc.winSize.width * 0.75,
5             cc.winSize.height * 0.5));
```

Then, fix these two bodies with a pivot joint to the default static body:

```
1   var staticBody=this.space.staticBody;
2
3   this.space.addConstraint(new cp.PivotJoint(bodyA, staticBody,
4      cc.p(cc.winSize.width * 0.25, cc.winSize.height * 0.5)));
5
6   this.space.addConstraint(new cp.PivotJoint(bodyB, staticBody,
7      cc.p(cc.winSize.width * 0.75, cc.winSize.height * 0.5)));
```

Then, apply simple motor to bodyA and bodyB:

```
1   var simpleMotor = new cp.SimpleMotor(bodyA, bodyB, Math.PI);
2   this.space.addConstraint(simpleMotor);
```

Here, the relative angular velocity of the two bodies is set to Math.PI. The following is the full source code of the layer:

```
1    var SimpleMotorLayer = BaseSampleLayer.extend({
2        sprite:null,
3        ctor:function () {
4            this._super();
5            this.initPhysics();
6            this.setupDebugNode();
7            this.addBottomWall();
8
9            var bodyA = this.addPhysicsBox(cc.p(cc.winSize.width * 0.25,
                 cc.winSiz\
10   e.height * 0.5));
```

```
11      var bodyB = this.addPhysicsBox(cc.p(cc.winSize.width * 0.75,
        cc.winSiz\
12      e.height * 0.5));

13

14      var staticBody=this.space.staticBody;

15

16      this.space.addConstraint(new cp.PivotJoint(bodyA, staticBody,
17      cc.p(cc.winSize.width * 0.25, cc.winSize.height * 0.5)));

18

19      this.space.addConstraint(new cp.PivotJoint(bodyB, staticBody,
20      cc.p(cc.winSize.width * 0.75, cc.winSize.height * 0.5)));

21

22      var simpleMotor = new cp.SimpleMotor(bodyA, bodyB, Math.PI);
23      this.space.addConstraint(simpleMotor);

24

25      this.scheduleUpdate();
26      return true;
27  },
28  initPhysics:function() {
29      //initiate space
30      this.space = new cp.Space();
31      //set up the Gravity
32      this.space.gravity = cp.v(0, -800); //Earth gravity
33      this.space.iterations = 30;
34      this.space.sleepTimeThreshold = Infinity;
35      this.space.collisionSlop = Infinity;
36  },

37

38  update:function (dt) {
39      this.space.step(dt);
40  },
41  addBottomWall: function() {
42      var bottomWall = new cp.SegmentShape(this.space.staticBody, new
        cp.v(0\
43      , 0), new cp.v(cc.winSize.width, 0), 5);
44      bottomWall.setElasticity(1);
45      bottomWall.setFriction(1);
46      this.space.addStaticShape(bottomWall);
47  },
48  setupDebugNode : function()
49  {
50      this._debugNode = new cc.PhysicsDebugNode(this.space);
51      this.addChild( this._debugNode );
52  },

53
```

```
54        addPhysicsBox: function(pos) {
55          var width=50,height=50,mass=1;
56          var phBodyBox = this.space.addBody(new cp.Body(mass,
            cp.momentForBox(m\
57          ass, width,height)));
58          phBodyBox.setPos(pos);
59
60          var phShape = this.space.addShape(new cp.BoxShape(phBodyBox,
            width, he\
61          ight));
62          phShape.setFriction(0);
63          phShape.setElasticity(1);
64          phShape.setCollisionType(1);
65
66          return phBodyBox;
67        }
68    });
```

You will see two boxes rotating at a constant speed, as in Figure 7-10.

Figure 7-10. Simple motor

7.9.9   Gear Joint

A gear joint is similar to simple motor, but a gear joint won't introduce the angular velocity by itself. Because the angular velocity of one body depends upon the other, the velocity depends on the ratio provided. Let's look at an example.

First, initialize the Chipmunk space and attach two boxes via a pivot joint to the static body, as in previous examples. In addition, add a third body, which is going to be bound with bodyB via a gear joint:

```
1   var bodyA = this.addPhysicsBox(cc.p(cc.winSize.width * 0.25,
2           cc.winSize.height * 0.5));
3   var bodyB = this.addPhysicsBox(cc.p(cc.winSize.width * 0.75,
4           cc.winSize.height * 0.5));
5   var bodyC = this.addPhysicsBox(cc.p(cc.winSize.width * 0.5,
6           cc.winSize.height * 0.3));
7   var staticBody=this.space.staticBody;
8
9   this.space.addConstraint(new cp.PivotJoint(bodyA, staticBody,
10      cc.p(cc.winSize.width * 0.25, cc.winSize.height * 0.5)));
11
12  this.space.addConstraint(new cp.PivotJoint(bodyB, staticBody,
13      cc.p(cc.winSize.width * 0.75, cc.winSize.height * 0.5)));
14
15  this.space.addConstraint(new cp.PivotJoint(bodyC, staticBody,
16      cc.p(cc.winSize.width * 0.5, cc.winSize.height * 0.3)));
```

Then, apply simple motor to bodyA and bodyB to introduce constant angular velocity:

```
1   var gearJoint = new cp.GearJoint(bodyB, bodyC, 0, 2);
2   this.space.addConstraint(gearJoint);
```

Then, apply a gear joint to bodyB and bodyC so that the bodyC rotation is dependent upon bodyB's angular velocity:

```
1   var gearJoint = new cp.GearJoint(bodyB, bodyC, 0, 2);
2   this.space.addConstraint(gearJoint);
```

The last two parameters are:

- offset - initial angular offset for two bodies
- ratio - ratio that velocity needs to maintain; in this case, angular velocity of bodyC is twice as slow as bodyB.

Here is the full source code of the layer:

```
1    var GearJointLayer = BaseSampleLayer.extend({
2        sprite:null,
3        ctor:function () {
4            this._super();
5            this.initPhysics();
6            this.setupDebugNode();
7            this.addBottomWall();
8
9            var bodyA = this.addPhysicsBox(cc.p(cc.winSize.width * 0.25,
             cc.winSiz\
10           e.height * 0.5));
11           var bodyB = this.addPhysicsBox(cc.p(cc.winSize.width * 0.75,
             cc.winSiz\
12           e.height * 0.5));
13           var bodyC = this.addPhysicsBox(cc.p(cc.winSize.width * 0.5,
             cc.winSize\
14           .height * 0.3));
15           var staticBody=this.space.staticBody;
16
17           this.space.addConstraint(new cp.PivotJoint(bodyA, staticBody,
18             cc.p(cc.winSize.width * 0.25, cc.winSize.height * 0.5)));
19
20           this.space.addConstraint(new cp.PivotJoint(bodyB, staticBody,
21             cc.p(cc.winSize.width * 0.75, cc.winSize.height * 0.5)));
22
23           this.space.addConstraint(new cp.PivotJoint(bodyC, staticBody,
24             cc.p(cc.winSize.width * 0.5, cc.winSize.height * 0.3)));
25
26           var simpleMotor = new cp.SimpleMotor(bodyA, bodyB, Math.PI);
27           this.space.addConstraint(simpleMotor);
28
29           var gearJoint = new cp.GearJoint(bodyB, bodyC, 0, 2);
30           this.space.addConstraint(gearJoint);
31
32           this.scheduleUpdate();
33           return true;
34       },
35       initPhysics:function() {
36           //initiate space
37           this.space = new cp.Space();
38           //set up the Gravity
39           this.space.gravity = cp.v(0, -800); //Earth gravity
40           this.space.iterations = 30;
41           this.space.sleepTimeThreshold = Infinity;
42           this.space.collisionSlop = Infinity;
43       },
```

```
44
45        update:function (dt) {
46          this.space.step(dt);
47        },
48        addBottomWall: function() {
49          var bottomWall = new cp.SegmentShape(this.space.staticBody, new
          cp.v(0\
50 , 0), new cp.v(cc.winSize.width, 0), 5);
51          bottomWall.setElasticity(1);
52          bottomWall.setFriction(1);
53          this.space.addStaticShape(bottomWall);
54        },
55        setupDebugNode : function()
56        {
57          this._debugNode = new cc.PhysicsDebugNode(this.space);
58          this.addChild( this._debugNode );
59        },
60
61        addPhysicsBox: function(pos) {
62          var width=50,height=50,mass=1;
63          var phBodyBox = this.space.addBody(new cp.Body(mass,
          cp.momentForBox(m\
64 ass, width,height)));
65          phBodyBox.setPos(pos);
66
67          var phShape = this.space.addShape(new cp.BoxShape(phBodyBox,
          width, he\
68 ight));
69          phShape.setFriction(0);
70          phShape.setElasticity(1);
71          phShape.setCollisionType(1);
72
73          return phBodyBox;
74      }
75 });
```

In the output you will see that box c rotates twice as slow as box b. See Figure 7-11.

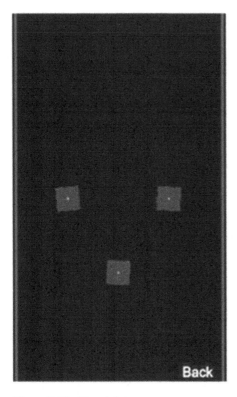

Figure 7-11. *Gear joint*

7.9.10   Ratchet Joint

The ratchet joint works like a socket wrench, where you have the body rotating in angular steps provided the initial angular offset, and phase is an angular step, which is the distance between the current and the next rotation steps.

Let's have look at the syntax:

```
1  var ratchet = new cp.RatchetJoint(body1, body2, offset, phase);
```

The parameters are as follows:

- offset - refers to the initial angular rotation of bodies
- phase - refers to the distance between steps

CHAPTER 8

■ ■ ■

Miscellaneous Features

8.1 Drawing Primitive Shapes

To draw primitive shapes, cc.drawNode is used. This node type has functions like drawCircle, drawPoly, drawRect, drawSegment, etc. Let's look at an example:

```
1   this.draw=new cc.DrawNode();
2   this.addChild(this.draw);
3
4   //drawCircle
5   this.draw.drawCircle(cc.p(cc.winSize.width / 2, cc.winSize.height / 2),
    100,\
6   0, 10, false, 6, cc.color(0, 255, 0, 255));
7   this.draw.drawCircle(cc.p(cc.winSize.width / 2, cc.winSize.height / 2),
    50, \
8   cc.degreesToRadians(90), 50, true, 2, cc.color(0, 255, 255, 255));
```

Here, two circles are drawn on the same DrawNode. You can draw any number of shapes on the same draw node. If you want to clear the shapes, you have use the clear function:

```
1   this.draw.clear();
```

Drawing a path is also possible using the drawCardinalSpline method:

```
1   this.draw.drawCardinalSpline(poinsArray,1,1,10,cc.color(255,255,255));
```

The first parameter is an array of points that define the path data. The second, third, and fourth parameters are tension, segment and line width, and line color, respectively.

Here is the full code:

```
1   var DrawNodeDemoLayer = BaseSampleLayer.extend({
2       sprite:null,
3       ctor:function () {
4
5           this._super();
```

© Hemanth Kumar 2016

H. Kumar and A. Rahman, *Rapid Game Development Using Cocos2d-JS*,

DOI 10.1007/978-1-4842-2553-0_8

```
6
7            var size = cc.winSize;
8
9            this.draw=new cc.DrawNode();
10           this.addChild(this.draw);
11
12           //drawCircle
13           this.draw.drawCircle(cc.p(size.width / 2, size.height / 2), 100,
             0, \
14   10, false, 6, cc.color(0, 255, 0, 255));
15           this.draw.drawCircle(cc.p(size.width / 2, size.height / 2), 50,
             cc.d\
16   egreesToRadians(90), 50, true, 2, cc.color(0, 255, 255, 255));
17
18           return true;
19       }
20   });
```

The output will look like Figure 8-1.

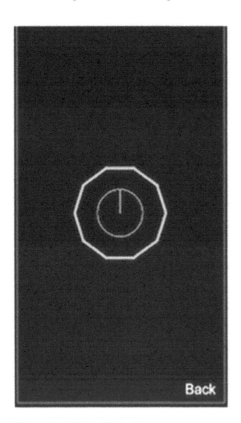

Figure 8-1. *DrawNode demo*

8.2   Adding Music and Sound Effects

In Cocos2d-js, music and sound effects can be added to the game by using the singleton object cc.audioEngine. Music represents the long-running background sound in your game, and sound effects represent quick sounds like the player jumping, collecting coins, etc. You have to be careful with which sound format file you use, as certain browsers won't support certain formats. The first thing you have to do during game startup is to pre-load your sound files during the onStart method of your app.js:

```
1   cc.audioEngine.preloadMusic(s_music_background);
2   cc.audioEngine.preloadEffect(s_music_jump);
```

Then, you can play your music and sound effects as follows:

```
1   cc.audioEngine.playMusic(s_music_background, true);
2   cc.audioEngine.playEffect(s_music_jump, true);
```

The second parameter represents whether to loop the sound or not.
You can pause, resume, and stop your music and effects as follows:

```
1   //Pause Sound
2   cc.audioEngine.pauseMusic();
3   cc.audioEngine.pauseEffect();
4
5   //Resume Sound
6   cc.audioEngine.resumeMusic();
7   cc.audioEngine.resumeEffect();
8
9   //Rewind Music
10  cc.audioEngine.rewindMusic();
11
12  //Stop Sound
13  cc.audioEngine.stopMusic();
14  cc.audioEngine.stopEffect();
```

For effects, there is no option to rewind, as the constructs for playing music and effects are separate so as to make the system efficient.

8.3   Using Custom Shaders

Shaders are responsible for rendering your whole game. Everything we do to run the game finally passes through these shaders and is processed for rendering. Shaders are classified into vertex and fragment shaders. Vertex shaders process the vertex data of your node and pass the output to fragment shaders, which process the pixel color for the interpolated vertex data. Cocos2d-x uses GL shaders to do the rendering. GL shaders are a much bigger concept, and discussing them in detail is out of scope of this book. Custom shaders are used to create cool effects in your game. We will see how to use custom vertex and fragment shaders on your sprite.

In Cocos2d-js, the cc.GLProgram class represents the shader entity for a particular node. Every node has setShaderProgram and getShaderProgram functions to get/set this object.

Let's consider sample vertex and fragment shaders:

```
1    //gray.vsh
2    attribute vec4 a_position;
3    attribute vec2 a_texCoord;
4    attribute vec4 a_color;
5
6
7    varying vec4 v_fragmentColor;
8    varying vec2 v_texCoord;
9
10   void main()
11   {
12       gl_Position = CC_MVPMatrix * a_position;
13       v_fragmentColor = a_color;
14       v_texCoord = a_texCoord;
15   }
16
17   //gray.fsh
18   varying vec4 v_fragmentColor;
19   varying vec2 v_texCoord;
20   uniform sampler2D CC_Texture0;
21
22   void main()
23   {
24           vec4 v_orColor = v_fragmentColor * texture2D(CC_Texture0, v_
             texCoord);
25           float gray = dot(v_orColor.rgb, vec3(0.299, 0.587, 0.114));
26           gl_FragColor = vec4(gray, gray, gray, v_orColor.a);
27   }
```

To use these shaders on your sprite, you would have to create a GLProgram instance and initiate it with these two shaders' paths, and you would have to initiate the attributes for the vertex shader. See the following:

```
1    var shader = new cc.GLProgram();
2    shader.retain();
3    shader.initWithFilenames("res/gray.vsh", "res/gray.fsh");
4    shader.addAttribute(cc.ATTRIBUTE_NAME_POSITION, cc.VERTEX_ATTRIB_
     POSITION);
5    shader.addAttribute(cc.ATTRIBUTE_NAME_COLOR, cc.VERTEX_ATTRIB_COLOR);
```

```
6   shader.addAttribute(cc.ATTRIBUTE_NAME_TEX_COORD, cc.VERTEX_ATTRIB_TEX_
    COORDS\
7   );
8
9   shader.link();
10  shader.updateUniforms();
11  this.sprite.setShaderProgram(shader);
```

8.4 Motion Trail Effect

In Cocos2d-js, a motion trail effect can be achieved through a class called MotionStreak. Motion trail effect is when an object moves and leaves traces of its path. The traces should fade away over time. It is like leaving behind footprints.

Let's look into an example. First, create an empty layer and add a sprite to it:

```
1   this.sprite = new cc.Sprite(res.Sprite_Image);
2   this.sprite.attr({
3       x: size.width / 2,
4       y: 0
5   });
6   this.addChild(this.sprite, 2);
```

Then, create an action and sequence combination that moves the sprite from bottom to top:

```
1   var action1 = cc.moveTo(5, cc.p(size.width / 2, size.height));
2   var action2= action1.reverse();
3   var seq1 = new cc.Sequence(action1,action2);
4   this.sprite.runAction(seq1.repeatForever());
```

Then, define the motion streak with a texture. It could be something very simple like a white triangle rotated to 90 degrees:

```
1   this.tail = new cc.MotionStreak(2, 3, 50, cc.color.WHITE, res.Tail);
2   this.tail.attr({
3       x: size.width / 2,
4       y: 0
5   });
6   this.addChild(this.tail,1);
```

The constructor of MotionStreak has the following parameters:

- fade - fade time of the trail
- minSeg - minimum number of segments
- stroke - stroke color of trail
- texture - image used to render the trail

The full source code of the layer should look like the following:

```
1   var MotionTrailLayer = BaseSampleLayer.extend({
2       sprite:null,
3       ctor:function () {
4           this._super();
5
6           var size = cc.winSize;
7
8           this.sprite = new cc.Sprite(res.Sprite_Image);
9           this.sprite.attr({
10              x: size.width / 2,
11              y: 0
12          });
13          this.addChild(this.sprite, 2);
14
15          var action1 = cc.moveTo(5, cc.p(size.width / 2, size.height));
16          var action2= action1.reverse();
17          var seq1 = new cc.Sequence(action1,action2);
18          this.sprite.runAction(seq1.repeatForever());
19
20          this.tail = new cc.MotionStreak(2, 3, 50, cc.color.WHITE, res.
            Tail);
21          this.tail.attr({
22              x: size.width / 2,
23              y: 0
24          });
25          this.addChild(this.tail,1);
26
27          var seq2 = seq1.clone();
28          this.tail.runAction(seq2.repeatForever());
29
30          return true;
31      }
32  });
```

And you will get the output seen in Figure 8-2.

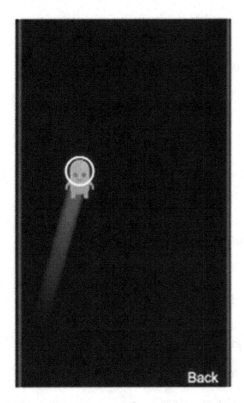

Figure 8-2. *Motion trail*

8.5 Accessing Local Storage

Local storage is nothing but the persistent storage facility offered by the platform (Web/Android/iOS) and is where you can store the key/value pair and retrieve it from later. Cocos2d-js offers an API to access the platform's local storage. You can use this API to store stuff like game state, user's high score, etc.

```
1   cc.sys.localStorage
```

The preceding object provides access to the local storage. There are two methods to get/set the values:

```
1   //set value to the localstorage
2   localstorage.setItem(<key>,<value>);
3
4   //get value from the localstorage
5   var value = localstorage.getItem(<key>);
```

The setItem method provides a way to set the value to the local storage using a key as reference. The key is a string, and the value could be a primitive value or a JavaScript object.

Let's have a look at a simple example. Create a new layer and, as in previous examples, add a label to the layer:

```
1   var size = cc.winSize;
2
3   this.Label = new cc.LabelTTF('','', 32);
4   this.Label.attr({
5       x: size.width / 2,
6       y: size.height / 2
7   });
8   this.addChild(this.Label);
```

Then, store a string value to local storage and retrieve it using var localstorage=cc.sys.localStorage:

```
1   //Store a key/value in localstorge
2   localstorage.setItem('key1','Text from localstorage');
3
4   //Retrieve value using key
5   var text=localStorage.getItem('key1');
```

The complete code should look like the following:

```
1    var LocalStorageLayer = BaseSampleLayer.extend({
2        sprite:null,
3        ctor:function () {
4
5            this._super();
6
7            var size = cc.winSize;
8
9            this.Label = new cc.LabelTTF('','', 32);
10           this.Label.attr({
11               x: size.width / 2,
12               y: size.height / 2
13           });
14           this.addChild(this.Label);
15
16           var localstorage=cc.sys.localStorage;
17
18           //Store a key/value in local storage
19           localstorage.setItem('key1','Text from localstorage');
20
```

```
21        var text=localStorage.getItem('key1');
22
23        //Retrive value using key in localStorage
24        this.Label.setString(text);
25
26        return true;
27    }
28 });
```

You will see the output shown in Figure 8-3.

Figure 8-3. *Local storage*

8.6 Schedule an Interval Callback

In Chapter 6, "Fun with Animation," we read about scheduler and updates, where every cc.Node can subscribe to the update notification, which is the run loop. Similarly, we can create a function to be called at a given interval of time. There is a function called schedule in cc.Node that does the job for us:

```
1   this.schedule(<callback>,<time>);
```

Let's have a look at an example. First, create an empty layer and add a label to it:

```
1   var size = cc.winSize;
2
3   this.Label = new cc.LabelTTF('','', 32);
4   this.Label.attr({
5       x: size.width / 2,
6       y: size.height / 2
7   });
8
9   this.addChild(this.Label);
```

Then, have a callback in the layer object and update the Label with text:

```
1   onUpdate:function(){
2       this.Label.setString((this.timer++)+' sec');
3   }
```

Then, have a variable timer initialized in ctor and use the schedule function to begin the callback with an interval of 1 second:

```
1   this.timer=0;
2   this.schedule(this.onUpdate,1);
```

Now the whole code should look like the following:

```
1    var SchedulerLayer = BaseSampleLayer.extend({
2        sprite:null,
3        ctor:function () {
4            this._super();
5
6            var size = cc.winSize;
7
8            this.Label = new cc.LabelTTF('','', 32);
9            this.Label.attr({
10               x: size.width / 2,
11               y: size.height / 2
12           });
13
```

```
14          this.addChild(this.Label);
15
16          this.timer=0;
17          this.schedule(this.onUpdate,1);
18
19          return true;
20      },
21      onUpdate:function(){
22          this.Label.setString((this.timer++)+' sec');
23      }
24  });
```

You will see the output shown in Figure 8-4.

Figure 8-4. Schedule a function

8.7 Accessing Current Language

Cocos2d-Js also provides a way to access the current locale in your runtime. There is a property in `cc.sys` where you can access the current language string:

```
1    cc.sys.language
```

Let's see a quick example. As in previous examples, add a label to an empty layer:

```
1    this.Label = new cc.LabelTTF('','', 32);
2    this.Label.attr({
3        x: size.width / 2,
4        y: size.height / 2
5    });
6
7    this.addChild(this.Label);
```

Then, access the language:

```
1    var language=cc.sys.language;
```

Then, set it to the label you added:

```
1    //set the language string
2    this.Label.setString('Current Locale: '+language);
```

Here is the full code:

```
var LanguageLayer = BaseSampleLayer.extend({ sprite:null, ctor:function ()
{ this._super();

1    var size = cc.winSize;
2
3    this.Label = new cc.LabelTTF('','', 32);
4    this.Label.attr({
5        x: size.width / 2,
6        y: size.height / 2
7    });
8
9    this.addChild(this.Label);
10
11   var language=cc.sys.language;
12
13   //set the language string
14   this.Label.setString('Current Locale: '+language);
15   return true;
16   }
17   });
```

You will get the output shown in Figure 8-5.

Figure 8-5. Accessing locale

8.8 Accessing System Capabilities

As you already know, your Cocos2d-js games can be deployed to different native platforms, which may have different capabilities. Cocos2d-js provides a way to detect the capabilities of the current environment through `cc.sys`:

```
1   cc.sys.capabilities
```

If you console this object in your browser, you will get an object structure like the following:

```
1   {
2       accelerometer: true,
3       canvas: true,
4       keyboard: true,
```

```
5      mouse: true,
6      opengl: true,
7    }
```

For example, if you want to detect if the system supports touch, you can simply query this object for the touch property. Similarly, other native capabilities can be queried.

8.9 Optimization

Optimization is a very crucial part of any kind of game. This is not the last process in your game development, however, as you have to plan ahead even before your coding process. There are certain tips and tricks that have been found to be best practices.

8.9.1 Memory Optimization

- Most of the memory in your game will be consumed by textures, so you have to pay closer attention to the size of the textures you are loading. Have a best practice of loading textures only when needed.

- Try to combine all the textures in your game into a sprite sheet or a texture atlas, as this will save you lot of memory.

- Also, it is good practice to always use NPOT textures instead of POT.

8.9.2 Performance Optimization

- When it comes to performance or the draw call's frame rate, delta time plays an important role.

- Make sure you avoid using a lot of draw calls. Use a single texture for all the sprites in your game, as this will enable sprite batching.

- Also, make sure you use SpriteBatchNode to combine all the needed sprites to be rendered in a single draw call if your platform doesn't support auto batching.

- If you write custom shaders, make sure your vertex and fragment shaders don't have any intensive operations.

- Having a complex computation in a shader will throttle the performance of the GPU, especially in fragment functions, since a fragment function will be executed for every pixel in your screen.

- Try to use 16-bit textures with RBGA4444 color depth.

8.9.3 JavaScript Level

- Make sure you have memory leak–free code.

- When you reference inner nodes maintained in outer nodes, make sure you clear the values when they are not needed.

- Use only documented APIs, as the usage and tweaking of internal variables and functions will lead to inconsistent behavior, as undocumented APIs are subject to changes in the upcoming versions.

8.10 Conclusion

So far, we have seen the features of Cocos2d-js from scratch. I hope this will give you a head start on your game development,. Cocos2d-x is big world, and a single book is not enough to explain all of its features in detail. We covered almost all of the features and advanced techniques as much as possible. It's time for you to create your own awesome game.

Index

© Hemanth Kumar 2016
H. Kumar and A. Rahman, *Rapid Game Development Using Cocos2d-JS*,
DOI 10.1007/978-1-4842-2553-0

Get the eBook for only $4.99!

Why limit yourself?

Now you can take the weightless companion with you wherever you go and access your content on your PC, phone, tablet, or reader.

Since you've purchased this print book, we are happy to offer you the eBook for just $4.99.

Convenient and fully searchable, the PDF version enables you to easily find and copy code—or perform examples by quickly toggling between instructions and applications.

To learn more, go to http://www.apress.com/us/shop/companion or contact support@apress.com.

Printed in the United States
By Bookmasters